Life in a Multi-lingual and Multi-cultural Society

グローバル時代の異文化コミュニケーション

朴シウォン
杉田めぐみ
小坂貴志
Daniel K. Goldner

KENKYUSHA

Life in a Multi-lingual and Multi-cultural Society

Copyright ©2013 by Siwon Park

Printed in Japan

まえがき

　以前，私がハワイに住んでいた頃，出張でニューヨークに行く機会がありました．長時間のフライトを終えてスーツケースを取り，JFK空港の外に出ると待っていたタクシーに乗り込み，会議が開かれる予定のホテルに向かいました．するとタクシーの運転手が私にどこから来たのかと尋ねてきました．私は何も考えずに「ハワイです」と答えると，私が日本人に見えたらしく，運転手は「てっきり日本から来たのかと思ったよ」と言いました．私が「といっても実は韓国人なんですけどね」と付け加えると，運転手は韓国大手企業のサムスンの話をし始めました．

　現在，私は日本に住んでいます．日本に来て8年が経ち，ようやく日本語で日常生活のほとんどのことをこなせるようになりました．以前は，自分の見た目が日本人と似ているというだけで，日本人のような日本語を話さなければならないというプレッシャーを感じていたこともありました．また，一人の英語教師として，自分の教え子たちの母国語を学ぶことは自分にとってごく自然なことだと思い，独学で日本語を勉強していた時期もありました．

　それから数年後，同僚の先生数人と共に仕事で韓国を訪れました．到着した次の日に簡単な市内観光をすることになり，当然ながら私がガイドをすることになりました．街の中心部で方向がわからなくなり，同僚たちが見守る中，バス停で学生らしき男性に道を尋ねました．その男子学生は一瞬私を見て，私が韓国語で質問しているにもかかわらず，なんと英語で質問に答えたのです．聞きたかった道順を知ることができたとはいえ，私が韓国語で質問したのになぜ彼が英語で答えたのか理解できませんでした．同僚たちは半分冗談で，「長く韓国を離れすぎたせいで，おかしな韓国語になってしまったのでは？」と言っていました．それを聞いて恥ずかしくもありましたが，確かに日本では韓国語を使う機会がほとんどないので，おそらくそれは事実だったのでしょう．自分は韓国人でありながら，母国の人から「韓国人」として見てもらえなかったという衝撃的なこの経験によって，私は今どこにいるのか，何をしているのか，自分が誰で，将来はどうなるのだろうかといったことについて深く考えるようになりました．

　本書は，複数の国，言語，文化に挟まれた環境に生きる人々に関する実際のストーリーです．私自身，多言語・多文化的な生活を送るようになって失った側面もある一方，得たものもたくさんあります．本書では，そのような多言語・多文化にまつわる経験から14のエピソードを Background Reading で紹介し，またその背景にどのような文化や価値観の違いが存在するのかを，Main Reading でやや専門的に説明しています．私自身が経験したように，皆さんにも本書を読んで何かを学んでもらえることを期待しています．

最後に，本書の執筆にあたりご協力いただいた多くの方に感謝申し上げます．特に，このテーマで英語テキストを執筆することを強く支援してくださった研究社の吉田尚志編集部長と，連日夜遅くまで，時には休日返上で編集作業に当たってくださった編集部の濱倉直子さんには心からお礼を申し上げます．

2013年9月20日
朴シウォン

目次

まえがき iii

各ユニットの構成 vi

UNIT 1 BECOMING MULTI-LINGUAL AND MULTI-CULTURAL 　[朴(P)] 2

UNIT 2 BACKGROUND MATTERS IN COMMUNICATION 　[GOLDNER (G)] 10

UNIT 3 NEVER LEARN WITHOUT TRYING 　[GOLDNER (G)] 18

UNIT 4 YOUNG KOREANS IN JAPAN 　[杉田(S)] 26

UNIT 5 WHEN SILENCE IS NOT GOLDEN 　[朴(P)] 34

UNIT 6 FLUENT BUT RUDE 　[朴(P)] 42

UNIT 7 JAPANESE AMERICANS 　[杉田(S)] 50

UNIT 8 THE FACE TALKS TOO! 　[朴(P)] 58

UNIT 9 THE V-SIGN WITH CHEESE 　[朴(P)] 66

UNIT 10 WHEN COURTESY FAILS 　[朴(P)] 74

UNIT 11 TO BECOME A REAL KOREAN 　[朴(P)] 82

UNIT 12 DOES AGE MATTER? 　[朴(P)] 90

UNIT 13 GREAT WAIT 　[小坂(K)] 98

UNIT 14 DIALOGUE IN AN AGE OF CONFLICT 　[小坂(K)] 106

GLOSSARY 114

編著者紹介 118

各ユニットの構成

1. Introduction

BACKGROUND READING

執筆者たちの実体験にまつわるエピソードを(自宅での)予習として自分で辞書を引きながら読んでおきます．

QUESTION

授業の最初にペアで議論することによって，トピックに対する自分の考えをまとめます．

2. Reading Focus

VOCABULARY STUDY

A. Matching: word and meaning
B. Word in Context

本文で使われる重要語句の意味を予習して，センテンスとして使用できるように練習します．

MAIN READING（本文）

知らない単語の意味を調べながら本文を読むことによって，読解力と語彙力を高めます．

READING CHECK

A. Comprehension
B. Key Ideas

本文の内容理解について確認するため，Aの選択問題（または空所補充選択問題）とBの空所補充問題を解きます．

3. Extension

LISTENING CHECK

本文の内容に関連した英文を聞いて，内容理解を確認するための選択問題に答えます．

Life in a Multi-lingual and Multi-cultural Society

グローバル時代の異文化コミュニケーション

UNIT 1: BECOMING MULTI-LINGUAL AND MULTI-CULTURAL

1. Introduction

BACKGROUND READING

Read the following story and answer the questions below with your partner.

> Whenever a new semester begins, students new to my classes ask me what I am, as if there's a quick answer to it. I just say that I'm a person who is, South Korean-born, educated in the U.S., and living in Japan. I know that's probably not the kind of answer they expected. They probably wanted more details from me, but I really don't know how I could introduce myself quickly in five minutes. Later when I become more intimate with them and find time to talk about something other than the contents that I'm supposed to cover, I tell my students how I see myself and what has formed me in my current self. Another question I'm often asked is how many languages I can speak. I answer quickly that I'm fluent in three languages and I know some other languages at a very surface level being a linguist and as a music major some years ago. Then, the response, "I envy you" (*iina*) comes from my students and they seem to be satisfied with my quick answer.
>
> We all have a relatively concrete understanding of being multi-lingual, but not of being multi-cultural, although they are the flip sides of a coin. To be multi-lingual, I had to become multi-cultural and as I became multi-cultural, I could become multi-lingual. However, living multi-lingual and multi-cultural has never been easy. Living in different countries and having been educated in institutions of different countries, it was necessary for me to undo many things that I once internalized. It is as if you were told to eat with your left hand even though you grew up right-handed. At first, you feel awkward and even find it upsetting, but you become ambidextrous as you try. When it comes to intercultural communication, it's like I'm ambidextrous, although not perfect, knowing how to use different languages with the appropriate cultural values and norms which help to deepen my understanding of my colleagues around the world.
>
> (P)

UNIT **1** BECOMING MULTI-LINGUAL AND MULTI-CULTURAL

QUESTION

1. Why do you think the author can't introduce himself quickly to his students in class?

2. Why does the author say becoming *multi-lingual* and *multi-cultural* is the flip sides of a coin?

3. Why does the author think he's ambidextrous in intercultural communication?

4. What does it mean to be *multi-lingual* and *multi-cultural* to you?
    - multi-lingual: _____
    - multi-cultural: _____

5. Of what language(s) and culture(s) would you want to become *multi-lingual* and *multi-cultural*, and why?

2. Reading Focus

VOCABULARY STUDY

A. Matching: word and meaning

Write the words in the blanks that match their meaning.

| immediately | recognize | subconscious | attention | complicated |
| realize | assumption | impose | notion | perspective |

1. _____ : the ability or the act to concentrate on a single object

2. _____ : to know or identify someone or something previously known or seen

3. _____ : a way of thinking about something or judging a situation; a view

4. _____ : without any delay

5. _____ : to force someone to accept something

6. _____ : something that is taken for granted; supposing

7. _____ : an idea; an opinion

8. _____ : to become aware or conscious of

9. _____ : existing or acting without awareness; below the level of consciousness

10. _____ : difficult to understand or explain

B. Word in Context

Fill in the blanks with the words from the list in Part A. Change the form of the words where necessary.

1. He has a _____ fear of snakes since he was a child.

2. It is a reasonable _____ that we will lose their support if our business doesn't benefit them.

3. They will _____ the importance of this policy when the economy actually gets better.

UNIT **1** BECOMING MULTI-LINGUAL AND MULTI-CULTURAL

4. No one can _____ his religious views on others. We all have the right to enjoy the freedom of religion and thought.

5. The _____ that the newspapers are disappearing due to the development of the Internet is not grounded on evidence.

6. He needs to pay more _____ to the lectures if he wants to pass the next exam.

MAIN READING

Read the text below and answer the following questions.

Undoing What Has Been Done

Once a Japanese student asked me what has made my life difficult in foreign countries. My answer was simple, "Undoing what had already been done." To help her to understand what I meant by "undoing," I asked her how she felt when she drove for the first time in the U.S. She immediately understood my point: When she drove in the U.S. for the first time, she had to remind herself to drive in the right lane until she got used to it.

As soon as we are born, we learn to deal with the patterns of the things around us. Through this pattern thinking, we can easily recognize and learn about colors, shapes, and even our first language with some biological support. Once patterns are learned, becoming part of our subconscious knowledge, we can recognize them without paying extra attention so that we can learn and do other things at the same time. It is as if we were riding a bicycle while doing things such as talking on our cell phone or text messaging. However, this supposedly advantageous psychological process sometimes works against us: It is difficult to switch it off even if we want to.

Read the expression on the right-hand side out loud.

THE MAP
figure 1

How did you read it? If you read it, as "THE MAP," did you notice the middle letters of the two words actually have the same shape? Although you read them differently; did you read one as H and

figure 2
Harper's Weekly, 19 November 1892 より

the other as A? Why? It's because your mind automatically applied your knowledge of the English language.

What makes things more complicated is the way we see things. There is a saying, "Seeing is believing," but what we see is not often the reality. Take a look at the picture on the left side quickly. What does it look like, a rabbit or a duck? Ask your classmates how they see it. You will find some saying a duck and others saying a rabbit: People see it differently at first glance. It's only when we pay closer attention to it that we realize it can look differently depending on where we focus.

We tend to see things differently depending on our previous experiences. Especially if we grew up in a different society with different cultural values and norms, it is rather natural to see things differently applying different assumptions. Living in a foreign country actually imposes similar psychological challenges to us. While we share a number of common values as human beings, we still find that we perceive things differently and impose different values on them. While differences in currency — the value of money — can easily be calculable and understandable, social and cultural values such as politeness, friendship, and even honesty may be considered different depending on where and how we grew up.

Since many of our cultural notions are subconscious, it is difficult for us to notice how our behaviors are seen by others of different cultures. Likewise, it is sometimes difficult to understand the behavior of others from different cultures because they act based on their own cultural values.

We see others and interpret their behaviors based on our cultural values, which have been internalized since we were born. But to live as a member of this fast-growing global society and to better understand our colleagues from other countries, we sometimes need to turn off our cultural thinking and see and interpret their behaviors through their own perspectives. Without such effort, we cannot expect the true meaning of cross-cultural communication to occur.

(P)

UNIT 1 BECOMING MULTI-LINGUAL AND MULTI-CULTURAL

Notes

- [7] get used to　～に慣れる
- [8] deal with　～に対処する
- [14] text messaging　(携帯電話での)メール交換
- [14] supposedly　いわゆる, ～と言われている
- [16] switch off　(電源を)切る, オフにする
- [20] actually　実際は
- [23] automatically　自動的に, 機械的に
- [31] at first glance　一目見ただけで
- [33] tend to　～しがちである, ～する傾向がある
- [33] previous　以前の, 先の
- [33] experience　経験
- [35] norm　規範, 規準
- [37] common values　共通価値, 共通認識
- [38] perceive　知覚する, 理解する
- [40] politeness　丁寧さ, 礼儀正しさ, ポライトネス
- [44] likewise　同様に
- [46] based on　～に基づいて
- [48] internalize　内面化する, 習得する
- [51] interpret　解釈する
- [52] cross-cultural communication　異文化コミュニケーション
- [52] occur　起こる, 発生する

READING CHECK

A. Comprehension

Answer the questions based on the reading.

1. What is the main topic of this reading?
    a. How the brain interprets the letters
    b. How to understand our own cultural norms correctly
    c. Why it's difficult to understand people from other cultures
    d. Why we need to automatize our thinking processes

2. Why did the author mention "driving" in Paragraph 1?
    a. To explain what "undoing" means
    b. To introduce his background
    c. To learn more about his student's background
    d. To let the student know the importance of driving

3. What lesson does "THE MAP" example teach us?
    a. We read the same letters differently depending on our cultural background.
    b. Many of our thinking processes are automatic.
    c. Reading ability requires automatic knowledge.
    d. We are often mistaken with English spellings.

4. What lesson does the author hope to introduce using the rabbit-duck picture?
    a. Our cultural background affects the way we perceive things.

b. In order to learn something, we need to pay attention to it first.
  c. The information we receive through our vision is often incorrect.
  d. We see things differently depending on where we focus.

5. Which of the following statements would the author agree with?
   a. Pattern thinking is a learning process mainly for adults.
   b. We must believe what we see more than what we are taught.
   c. It is easy to notice how other people apply their own cultural values to their behaviors.
   d. People's behaviors must be understood based on their own cultural backgrounds.

B. Key Ideas

Without looking back, complete the sentences with the words in the parentheses. Change the form of the words where necessary.

1. (   ) this pattern thinking, we can easily recognize and (   ) about colors, (   ), and even our first (   ) with some (   ) support.
   (shape, language, through, biology, learn)

2. Once (   ) are learned, becoming part of our subconscious (   ), we can (   ) them without paying extra (   ) so that we can learn and do other things (   ).
   (at the same time, knowledge, attention, pattern, recognize)

3. While we (   ) a number of (   ) values as human (   ), we still find that we (   ) things differently and (   ) different values on them.
   (perceive, share, impose, being, common)

4. Since many of our (   ) notions are (   ), it is difficult for us to (   ) how our (   ) are seen by others of (   ) cultures.
   (subconscious, different, behavior, notice, cultural)

5. To live as a (   ) of this fast-growing (   ) society and to better understand our colleagues from other countries, we sometimes need to (   ) our (   ) thinking and see and interpret their behaviors through their own (   ).
   (global, member, perspective, turn off, cultural)

8

UNIT **1** BECOMING MULTI-LINGUAL AND MULTI-CULTURAL

3. Extension

LISTENING CHECK

Listen to a talk and answer the following questions.

1. Which of the following countries has the speaker NOT lived in?
   a. Korea
   b. Japan
   c. Canada
   d. The U.S.

2. According to the speaker, how has he been changed, after living in different countries?
   a. He can speak more languages.
   b. He has become more sensitive to cultural differences.
   c. He can keep the right manner depending on the place.
   d. He has become less conscious of other people.

3. According to the speaker, about what does he sometimes wonder?
   a. Why there are different countries in the world
   b. Why people speak different languages
   c. Why people of different cultures keep the same manner
   d. Why people like to travel and meet different people

4. According to the talk, which of the following is true about the speaker?
   a. He is now living in Japan.
   b. He visited his parents in America last winter.
   c. He didn't like to use a fork when he ate his meals in the U.S.
   d. His parents were happy about his manner when he met them last time.

UNIT 2: BACKGROUND MATTERS IN COMMUNICATION

1. Introduction

BACKGROUND READING

Read the following story and answer the questions below with your partner.

I once met a man from India in of all places, Korea. He was a book publishing representative. Our meeting took place at his office in the busy city of Seoul. As I sat in his office listening attentively to his sales pitch, I was shocked and upset by his lack of attention to our meeting. While conversing with me, he was constantly checking his cell phone and giving directives to the secretaries in the secretarial pool outside his office. I tried to hide my disappointment at what I considered to be his rude behavior. I told myself that this kind of multi-tasking is necessary for a man in his position and field of work. I come from a small town in Michigan, USA, where the pace of life is slower; I always found it to be stressful living in Seoul, a huge city of 10 million people. Every day, I had to deal with the sea of people bumping into me as we crossed paths without even an apology. I thought these people from India and Korea were so rude. This was my introduction to *¹polychronic cultures.

Cross-cultural communication is like a mine field — filled with the potential for disaster with every misstep. It's difficult enough to get along with people from your own culture let alone throwing different languages, cultures, and expectations into the mix. The anthropologist *²Edward T. Hall is considered to be the father of cross-cultural communication. Among his theories is the concept of polychronic vs. *³monochronic communication. In polychronic cultures such as India, Korea, and Japan, people like to engage in multiple tasks at the same time. They are used to having an abundance of stimuli and can separate the most pressing needs while ignoring all the others for that moment. People from monochronic cultures, like the U.S., tend to do better with one task at a time.

(G)

*1 polychronic　多元的に時間を使う〈文化〉
*2 Edward T. Hall　エドワード T. ホール (1914-2009)《米国の文化人類学者》
*3 monochronic　単一的に時間を使う〈文化〉

UNIT **2** BACKGROUND MATTERS IN COMMUNICATION

QUESTION

1. What do you think the author was upset about with the Indian publisher?

2. How does the author compare his hometown with Seoul?

3. How does he describe cross-cultural communication?

4. How are polychronic individuals different from monochronic individuals?

5. Are you a polychronic person or a monochronic person and why do you think so?

2. Reading Focus

VOCABULARY STUDY

A. Matching: word and meaning

Write the words in the blanks that match their meaning.

| avoid | destination | vital | furious | intercultural |
| straightforward | concept | dichotomy | interlocutor | explicit |

1. _____ : direct; honest

2. _____ : to keep away from

3. _____ : an abstract idea

4. _____ : fully and clearly expressed

5. _____ : division into two parts

6. _____ : very important or necessary

7. _____ : extremely angry

8. _____ : involving different cultures

9. _____ : a place to which someone is going

10. _____ : someone who you are having a conversation with

B. Word in Context

Fill in the blanks with the words from the list in Part A. Change the form of the words where necessary.

1. She gave me _____ instructions on how to prepare handouts for the meeting.

2. English classes are a _____ part of our university's curriculum.

3. The interviewer will want a _____ answer as to what you are good at.

4. Learning a foreign language also promotes _____ understanding.

5. How did people first accept the _____ of "freedom of speech" in the U.S.?

6. The president was very brave to propose a new health care plan. He didn't want to _____ the possible blame he could receive from the people of the opposite party.

UNIT **2** BACKGROUND MATTERS IN COMMUNICATION

MAIN READING

Read the text below and answer the following questions.

Are You Hungry?

Have you ever made a mistake but didn't know what you did that was wrong? It's hard to avoid making mistakes if you're not aware of the problem in the first place. This occurs frequently in cross-cultural communications. What is considered the norm or acceptable in one culture can have a completely different meaning in another.

I've made many a blunder in my various cross-cultural interactions, but one in particular stands out. When I was an undergraduate student, I had a Japanese girlfriend. One day in late autumn, we had plans for a weekend camping trip at my parents' cabin in northern Michigan with the rest of my family. After my Friday morning class, I rushed to pack everything into my car and picked up my girlfriend. In my eagerness to get to the cabin, I thought we could eat a late lunch once we reached our destination.

About thirty minutes into our drive, she asked me, "Are you hungry?" Without even thinking about it, I said, "No, how about you?" When she replied, "No," I just put the 'pedal to the metal' and kept on driving as fast as I could legally get away with. By the time we arrived at the cabin, I had made the usual three hour drive in less than two and a half hours. I was pleased with my driving skill and was looking forward to an enjoyable meal. However, as soon as I had parked the car, she got out and slammed the door with a furious thud.

I sat in the car for a while trying to figure out why she was mad, and what I might have done to make her so mad. I was totally dumbfounded. When her anger had subsided enough to speak to me, she explained what I had done wrong. It turned out that when she asked me if I was hungry, it should be 'implied' that she was hungry. Later, when I took an Intercultural Communication class, I instantly recognized this situation in one of the concepts of the course.

Edward T. Hall was one of the first to write about the dichotomy between a high-context culture like Japan, Korea, China, and many Latin American countries and a low-context culture like the U.S. and many European countries. In a high-context culture, the context of the situation and the relationship of the interlocutors play a vital role in the message being communicated; hence, a few words can communicate a very complex message. Conversely, in a low-context culture, everything is direct, straightforward, and individualistic, often times to the point of redundancy; if you listen to an American lecturer, he will tell you what he's going to talk about, then talk about it, and when he has finished, will tell you what he just talked about!

Our problem arose because I, coming from a low-context culture, asked a question, "… how about you?" and when I received the explicit response, "No," I took that at its face value, not considering the time of day — around noon; nor my girlfriend's expectation that we usually eat lunch around this time. I was more focused on completing the task of getting to the cabin; whereas, she was expecting a nice trip on the way to the cabin.

Looking back on that incident, after she asked if I was hungry, I should have noticed that she didn't say a single word to me during the entire drive up to the cabin. Ignorance is no excuse, but it can be forgiven, inattentiveness, on the other hand, cannot.

(G)

Notes

[3] be aware of 〜に気づく	[22] dumbfound 唖然とさせる
[7] make a blunder へまをする	[23] subside 和らぐ, 落ち着く
[7] interaction 意思の伝えあい, 交流; 相互作用	[28] context コンテクスト, 文脈, 背景
[8] stand out 際立つ	[31] play a role 役割をになう
[12] in one's eagerness to 〜したさのあまり	[32] conversely 反対に
[16] put the pedal to the metal 車を全速力で運転する	[39] at its face value 額面どおりに
	[45] no excuse 弁解の余地がない
[21] figure out 理解する	[45] inattentiveness 配慮が足りないこと, 無神経

UNIT **2** BACKGROUND MATTERS IN COMMUNICATION

READING CHECK

A. Comprehension

Answer the questions based on the reading.

1. What is the main topic of this reading?
    a. Gender difference in communication
    b. How context affects the way people talk
    c. Why talking is better than keeping silent
    d. How speakers' culture affects their communication

2. According to the reading, which of the following is true about the author?
    a. He never experienced cross-cultural misunderstandings.
    b. He didn't know why his girlfriend got angry the first time.
    c. His girlfriend was an American.
    d. He was not happy with his driving skills.

3. Which of the following countries is mentioned as an example of the high-context culture?
    a. America   b. European countries
    c. Canada   d. Japan

4. According to the reading, which of the following may NOT be a characteristic of the low-context culture?
    a. Straightforward   b. Implicit
    c. Direct   d. Individualistic

5. What does the underlined statement mean in the last paragraph?
    a. Inattentiveness can be an excuse for ignorance.
    b. If you pay attention, you won't be ignorant.
    c. To not know something is okay, but to not pay attention is not okay.
    d. If you are stupid, you will be considered rude.

B. Key Ideas

Without looking back, complete the sentences with the words in the parentheses. Change the form of the words where necessary.

1. What is (   ) the (   ) or acceptable in one (   ) can have a completely different (   ) in another.
    (norm, meaning, consider, culture)

15

2. When I took an (　　) Communication class, I instantly (　　) this (　　) in one of the (　　) of the course.

  (concept, intercultural, situation, recognize)

3. In a (　　) culture, the context of the situation and the (　　) of the interlocutors play a (　　) role in the (　　) being communicated.

  (vital, relationship, high-context, message)

4. In a (　　) culture, (　　) is (　　), straightforward, and individualistic, often times to the point of (　　).

  (everything, direct, low-context, redundancy)

5. I was more (　　) on (　　) the task of (　　) to the cabin; whereas, she was (　　) a nice trip on the way to the cabin.

  (expect, get, complete, focus)

3. Extension

LISTENING CHECK

Listen to a talk and answer the following questions.

1. What is the speaker's occupation in Japan?
   - a. A university student
   - b. A university lecturer
   - c. A manager of a dormitory
   - d. An administrative worker

2. What was surprising to the speaker about the Japanese university?
   - a. Students don't know where to find information.
   - b. Teachers give explicit information to the students.
   - c. Students seem to know what they are supposed to do without instruction.
   - d. The university keeps the campus very clean.

3. Which of the following is true about the speaker?
   - a. He thinks American universities are dirty.
   - b. He studied in a Japanese university.
   - c. He often tells his students to be quiet in the classroom.
   - d. He thinks American students receive more explicit information than Japanese ones.

UNIT 2 BACKGROUND MATTERS IN COMMUNICATION

4. What did the speaker learn from his experiences with the American and Japanese universities?
    a. How similar high- and low-context cultures are
    b. How different cultures affect people's expectation
    c. Why American university students frequently check the bulletin boards
    d. Why the Japanese professor complained about current Japanese students

UNIT 3 NEVER LEARN WITHOUT TRYING

1. Introduction

BACKGROUND READING

Read the following story and answer the questions below with your partner.

When I was a graduate student in Hawaii, I taught at a Japanese junior college. We would have a new group of freshmen students from Japan arrive every fall semester. They all came to the U.S. with very limited listening and speaking abilities in English. One class in particular comes to mind. In this class, there were two very hard working female students who studied all the time, and this one other female student, who didn't study as much. The two studious girls were just your average-looking, shy Japanese girls; whereas, the non-studious one was very attractive and outgoing.

As the semester neared its end, it became very apparent that there was a difference in the listening and speaking skills of these girls. The two shy girls had spent most of their time in the school's building studying by themselves in the library. This school had only one big building with parking space on the lower levels, office and administration on the next level, followed by classrooms and finally dormitory rooms on the top level. These girls never had to leave the building if they didn't want to, and it seemed as though they rarely did. As a result, their speaking skills moved along at very small increments. In contrast, the outgoing girl had spent all of her time hanging out at the beach and partying with her native English speaking surfer boyfriends, and her speaking skills skyrocketed [*1]off the charts, much to the displeasure of her two classmates.

The moral is that the smart girls approached their learning of English in much the same way as they had for all of their academic courses, but without much success; whereas, the talkative girl made significant improvements in her English by means of immersing herself in the local environment and actually using the language to communicate.

(G)

*1 off the charts 飛びぬけて

UNIT **3** NEVER LEARN WITHOUT TRYING

QUESTION

1. Among the Japanese students the author taught which one improved English listening and speaking skills and why?

2. What may have been a problem with how the two shy Japanese girls studied English?

3. What are the lessons that the author hopes to deliver in the reading about foreign language learning?

4. Do you know anyone who seemed to have made a lot of progress in English proficiency in a short period of time? How did he study English?

5. What are good ways to learn English speaking in your own understanding?

2. Reading Focus

VOCABULARY STUDY

A. Matching: word and meaning

Write the words in the blanks that match their meaning.

| fundamental | appropriateness | intellect | acquire | superiority |
| detrimental | utterance | hinder | embarrassment | interact |

1. _____ : to gain knowledge or skills; to learn
2. _____ : the quality of being superior
3. _____ : something said; speech
4. _____ : the ability to learn; intellectual ability
5. _____ : the shame you feel when something has gone wrong by your mistake
6. _____ : doing the right thing; right behavior
7. _____ : basic; essential
8. _____ : damaging; harmful
9. _____ : to communicate with or respond to someone; to act together
10. _____ : to get in the way of; to prevent

B. Word in Context

Fill in the blanks with the words from the list in Part A. Change the form of the words where necessary.

1. We are looking for a new teammate who can _____ with other members well.

2. There is a _____ difference between child language acquisition and adult language acquisition.

3. We must never encourage our friends to smoke because smoking can be very _____ to our health.

4. The actor was very _____ by the reporter's questions about his private life.

5. She confessed there were times when she felt being a woman _____ her professional development as a politician.

6. Parents forget too often that they serve to model _____ behaviors for their children.

MAIN READING

Read the text below and answer the following questions.

Trash Luggage

There is a fundamental difference between how children and adults learn a second language (L2). In most cases, a child can master an L2 quite easily, whereas an adult typically fails in their acquisition of an L2. This seems counterintuitive, since the adult has already mastered their first language (L1), has a higher intellect, and more life experiences. By all accounts, the adult should be better than the child at acquiring an L2, just as they are better at most things. What is usually a benefit for adult superiority over children is actually detrimental for L2 acquisition: The adult, with the higher intellect, thinks too much.

This thinking leads to over-analyzing L2 acquisition; they think about all the grammatical rules and the pragmatic appropriateness of an utterance, to the point that it hinders any real communicative competence. Children, on the other hand, are too busy playing with their native-speaking friends, and don't let language get in the way of their fun. They are not embarrassed at making mistakes. Adults could learn something from children when it comes to learning a second language; most significantly, not to let the embarrassment of making mistakes interfere with their L2 acquisition.

I, too, have been guilty of letting my ego interfere with my L2 acquisition. I took a Korean language class at the university while I was in Hawaii, but never practiced my Korean outside of the classroom because I was afraid of making mistakes and looking stupid. I vowed not to let that inhibit me from learning Korean when I accepted a teaching position in Korea. On my first full day in Korea, I took a leisurely stroll around my new neighborhood just to get a sense of the environment and to purchase a few necessities.

Before going back to my apartment, I decided to step into the local convenience store to buy some snacks, an adapter plug for my laptop, and trash bags. I easily found everything I needed except for the trash bags. I searched all the shelves repeatedly but to no avail. I was dreading this, but I would have to ask the clerk; my first utterance in Korean.

As I hesitantly approached the counter, I felt confident that I knew the basic Korean word for trash (*suhraygi*) and the word for bag (*kabang*). So I asked the clerk, a young college co-ed, in my best Korean pronunciation, "*Shille hamnida, suhraygi kabang issoyo*?" (Excuse me, do you have trash bags?). This young lady gave me a puzzled look and a slight giggle but then reached down and handed me some plastic trash bags. Success! I had achieved my desired task. I paid for my things and as I was walking out of the store, I read the Korean words on the trash bag. It said, "*suhraygi bongtu*." No wonder the clerk had giggled. As I learned later, "*bongtu*" is the word for vinyl bags or what I know in the U.S. as plastic bags and "*kabang*" is the word for larger things like suitcases. Apparently, I had asked the clerk for "trash luggage."

By not being inhibited by my fear of making mistakes, I was able to successfully interact in my L2 and learn a new word on my first day in Korea and in my very first interaction. I wish I could say that all of my interactions in Korea were as successful, but it wasn't because I let embarrassment get in the way.

(G)

UNIT **3** NEVER LEARN WITHOUT TRYING

Notes

[3] second language　第二言語
[4] counterintuitive　反直観的
[6] by all accounts　誰から聞いても
[11] pragmatic　語用上の
[12] communicative competence　コミュニケーション能力
[14] get in the way of　〜の障害になる
[15] when it comes to　〜について言えば
[17] interfere with　〜の妨げとなる
[21] inhibit 〜 from …　〜に…させない
[23] take a leisurely stroll around　近所をゆっくり散歩する

[28] but to no avail　その甲斐なく
[28] dread　ひどく怖がる
[31] *suhraygi*　쓰레기 ((「ゴミ」の意の韓国語))
[31] *kabang*　가방 ((「カバン」の意の韓国語))
[32] *Shille hamnida*　실례합니다 ((「すみませんが、失礼ですが」の意の韓国語))
[33] *issoyo?*　있어요? ((「〜ありますか？」の意の韓国語))
[37] *suhraygi bongtu*　쓰레기 봉투 ((「ゴミ袋」の意の韓国語))

READING CHECK

A. Comprehension

Answer the questions based on the reading.(Choose the best answer to complete the sentence.)

1. What is the main topic of this reading?
    a. What the similarities are between L1 and L2 learning
    b. How adults' L2 learning is different from children's L2 learning
    c. Why it's difficult for adults to learn an L2
    d. Why it's important to try in L2 learning

2. According to the reading, which of the following is true about the author?
    a. He attended a university in Korea.
    b. He took a Korean class at his university.
    c. He never worried about making mistakes when he spoke Korean.
    d. He practiced his Korean very hard before he went to Korea.

3. Which of the following did the author not want to buy on the way back to his apartment?
    a. Snacks   b. An adapter plug
    c. Luggage   d. Trash bag

4. The author could find everything at the convenience store except for _____.
    a. Snacks   b. An adapter plug
    c. Luggage   d. Trash bag

5. Which of the following statements would the author agree with?
    a. Adults can learn an L2 better than children.
    b. Making mistakes in learning L2 is not good.
    c. We need a strong ego when we learn an L2.
    d. In L2 learning, we must not be afraid of feeling embarrassed.

B. Key Ideas

Without looking back, complete the sentences with the words in the parentheses. Change the form of the words where necessary.

1. There is a (   ) (   ) between how children and (   ) learn a (   ) language.
    (adult, difference, fundamental, second)

2. What is usually a (   ) for adult (   ) over children is actually (   ) for L2 (   ).
    (benefit, acquisition, superiority, detrimental)

3. Children, on the (   ) hand, are too busy (   ) with their native-speaking friends, and don't (   ) language get in the (   ) of their fun.
    (let, way, play, other)

4. On my first full day in Korea, I took a (   ) stroll around my new (   ) just to get a (   ) of the environment and to (   ) a few necessities.
    (sense, leisure, purchase, neighborhood)

5. By (   ) being (   ) by my (   ) of making mistakes, I was able to successfully (   ) in my L2.
    (fear, interact, inhibit, not)

UNIT 3 NEVER LEARN WITHOUT TRYING

3. Extension

LISTENING CHECK

Listen to a talk and answer the following questions.

1. What does the ROF in ROFLOL mean?
   a. Lolling on the floor
   b. Rolling on the floor
   c. Rocking on the floor
   d. Falling on the floor

2. According to the speaker, what is his wife's best quality?
   a. She is thoughtful.
   b. She is funny.
   c. She is beautiful.
   d. She is smart.

3. According to the talk, what kind of animal was his wife imitating?
   a. A kangaroo
   b. A cat
   c. A jaguar
   d. A mongoose

4. According to the talk, which of the following is true about the speaker?
   a. He is laughing regularly.
   b. He likes good medicine.
   c. He met his wife when he was a child.
   d. He cries all the time.

UNIT 4 YOUNG KOREANS IN JAPAN

1. Introduction

BACKGROUND READING

Read the following story and answer the questions below with your partner.

I once took a Korean class at a university in America. There was a student from Miyagi prefecture taking the same class. He was a young "*Zainichi Kankokujin*" and was called by his Korean name during the class. I thought that was the only name he had even though he was from Japan and his first language was Japanese. But later he told me it was only after he moved to the U.S. that he started using his Korean name — until then, he hated the fact that his "real" name was Korean and went by his Japanese name. As an example, one day my friend went to the driver's license center in Japan to renew his license. It is always the case that they call out the driver's name when his new license is ready for pickup. My friend's real name, which is a Korean name, was also called out loudly in front of everyone. Not feeling comfortable, he rushed to the pickup counter and immediately left there, he said.

My friend didn't go through any severe discrimination or "*ijime*" in Japan because of his Korean background. Yet, he didn't want to live as a Korean probably because he was born and raised in Japan, and spoke only Japanese, just like other Japanese. In a sense, his identity as "Japanese" was dominant. After he moved to the U.S., where various ethnic groups including Koreans and Japanese coexist, his identity as Korean became evident. This led to him taking a Korean class at an American university, although it was not his major. To my eyes, he looked more positive about his life than when he was living in Japan. He was obviously enjoying his life as a Korean, although he never denied his life in Japan.

Then I wondered what identity he would have the next time he went back to Japan — Korean or Japanese?

(S)

UNIT **4** YOUNG KOREANS IN JAPAN

QUESTION

1. Why do you think the author's friend at first hated the fact that his "real" name is Korean?

2. Why do you think the author's friend's identity changed after moving to the U.S.?

3. What may be the reason(s) that the author's friend decided to study Korean?

4. What do you think made the author's friend "more positive" about his life in the U.S.?

5. How do you think the author's friend would feel about his identity next time he went back to Japan?

2. Reading Focus

VOCABULARY STUDY

A. Matching: word and meaning

Write the words in the blanks that match their meaning.

| inferiority | attain | establish | register | oppose |
| encounter | conflict | overcome | assimilate | feature |

1. _____ : to sign one's name on; to record formally
2. _____ : to go or stand against
3. _____ : the state of being lower in rank, status, or value
4. _____ : to get through; to get over
5. _____ : to bring something into existence
6. _____ : a struggle with a differing idea or position; disagreement
7. _____ : to become familiar with or part of; to conform
8. _____ : to gain; to achieve
9. _____ : a noticeable quality of something; a characteristic
10. _____ : to meet (with); to run into

B. Word in Context

Fill in the blanks with the words from the list in Part A. Change the form of the words where necessary.

1. The immigrants tried to _____ themselves with the people in the neighborhood.
2. It is obvious that you and I have _____ points of view.
3. We should study the geographical _____ of the country before we visit there.
4. The doctor will give you some advice on how to get rid of a sense of _____.
5. Have you _____ for the new language program yet?
6. The owner of the company has _____ great success.

UNIT **4** YOUNG KOREANS IN JAPAN

MAIN READING

Read the text below and answer the following questions.

Identity of Young Koreans in Japan

The term "identity" was first used in the 1950's by Erik H. Erikson, an American scholar in the field of developmental psychology. He was born and raised in Germany, where he was often discriminated against because of his Jewish background. In addition, throughout his life, he never knew who his father was. Such personal experiences made him wonder who he was, where he belonged, how he should live, etc. — those questions related to the concept of "identity." According to Erikson, all human beings encounter, at some point of their lives, a situation in which one questions himself about who he is. In developmental psychology, it is a necessary step in the process of establishing the sense of "self."

Ethnic minority groups such as Koreans in Japan, however, experience a particular process because of historical, social, and political reasons. They are born and raised in Japan just like other Japanese, and their lifestyles are no different from those of other Japanese families. It is not unusual that parents do not tell their children about their Korean background until they become adults. Many young Koreans, who have assimilated with other Japanese, get quite shocked when they face the fact that they actually belong to a different ethnic group from their friends or people around them.

Lee (1999) suggests the following four stages for the developmental process of identity of young Koreans assimilated with other Japanese.

1. They do not know their Korean background. Some of them find out that they are not Japanese when they need to register as foreigner residents at the age of 16.
2. Some of them experience prejudice or discrimination, which may lead to the feeling of inferiority to other Japanese. They may try to hide their background and pretend to be Japanese.

3. They decide to tell the truth to their close friends or use their Korean names instead of Japanese names. They recognize themselves overcoming the inferior feelings.
4. They attain their own identity and discover their own way to live in the society.

Fukuoka and Tsujiyama (1991) further propose four types in the last stage of "identity attainment."

Type A: Trying to live as "*Zainichi*" in harmony with Japanese
Type B: Trying to live as Koreans (not as "*Zainichi*") in Japan
Type C: Trying to live as individuals, neither as Koreans nor Japanese
Type D: Trying to live as Japanese (just like other Japanese)

No one lives in exactly the same environment as others and everyone has a different idea about how he wants to live. So it is understandable that we cannot presume that all young Koreans have a similar idea as to how they want to live in Japanese society.

Fukuoka (1993) also points out two facts which cause mental conflicts for young Koreans in Japan. The first fact is that they assimilate themselves with other Japanese in the society with no intention. They were raised in Japan, growing up with Japanese values and speaking Japanese as their mother tongue, which was very natural for them. The second fact is that although they grew up in Japanese society, there is something different about them — ethnicity, way of thinking, family traditions, etc. There are some features of "disassimilated self" in themselves. These two opposing aspects make it difficult for young Koreans in Japan to find out "Who I am" or "Where I should go."

The male student in the Korean class might be back in Japan, or he might have decided to live in America or Korea. No matter where he lives, he must by now have a clearer sense of identity and a positive idea about how he would live. Identity is not something given to you, but something you create, develop, and change through interacting with other people around you.

(S)

UNIT **4** YOUNG KOREANS IN JAPAN

> **Notes**
>
> [2] term　用語
> [2] Erik H. Erikson　エリク H. エリクソン（1902-94）《ドイツ生まれの米国の精神分析家》
> [3] developmental psychology　発達心理学
> [12] ethnic　民族の，人種の
> [12] experience　経験する
> [14-15] no different from　～と全く変わらない
> [20] Lee (1999)　李洙任（1999）「変わりつつある在日韓国・朝鮮人のエスニック・アイデンティティ」『大阪女学院短期大学紀要』第29号
> [23] resident　住民
> [27] pretend to　～のふりをする
> [32] Fukuoka and Tsujiyama (1991)　福岡安則・辻山ゆき子（1991）『同化と異化のはざまで─在日若者世代のアイデンティティ葛藤』新幹社
> [34] in harmony with　～と調和して
> [42] Fukuoka (1993)　福岡安則（1993）『在日韓国・朝鮮人──若い世代のアイデンティティ』（中公新書），中央公論社
> [42] mental conflict　心の葛藤
> [44] intention　意図，意志
> [45] mother tongue　母国語，母語
> [47] ethnicity　民族意識，民族性
> [48] disassimilated self　異化された自己
> [52] No matter where he lives　彼がどこに住もうと

READING CHECK

A. Comprehension

Answer the questions based on the reading. (Choose the best answer to complete the sentence.)

1. What is true about Erik H. Erikson?
    a. He was raised by his American father.
    b. He developed a theory of identity based on his personal history.
    c. He suggests that it is possible for people to lose the sense of "self."
    d. He was accused of discriminating against Jewish people.

2. The lifestyles of Koreans in Japan are _____.
    a. understood well by Japanese
    b. imitated by Japanese
    c. similar to those of Japanese
    d. simpler than those of Japanese

3. The developmental process suggested by Lee (1999) shows _____.
    a. how young Koreans become aware of their ethnic identity
    b. how Japanese assimilate themselves to Koreans in Japan
    c. how Japanese and Koreans interact with each other
    d. how Korean parents tell their children about their identity

4. According to Fukuoka (1993), why do young Koreans in Japan experience "mental conflicts"?
   a. Because they are more sensitive than other ethnic groups in Japan.
   b. Because they are young and easy to be affected by others.
   c. Because they are different from older generations of Koreans in Japan.
   d. Because they are born in a situation with some factors which cannot be controlled.

5. The author thinks the male student in the Korean class _____.
   a. is now living in Korea
   b. must be more confident about his life
   c. must have a different identity
   d. might change his name again

B. Key Ideas

Without looking back, complete the sentences with the words in the parentheses. Change the form of the words where necessary.

1. He was (   ) and raised in Germany, where he was often (   ) against (   ) of his (   ) background.
   (discriminate, Jew, bear, because)

2. According to Erikson, all human beings (   ), at some (   ) of their lives, a (   ) in which one (   ) himself about who he is.
   (question, encounter, point, situation)

3. Many young Koreans, who have (   ) with other Japanese, get quite shocked when they (   ) the fact that they actually (   ) to a different (   ) group from their friends or people around them.
   (belong, assimilate, ethnic, face)

4. So it is (   ) that we cannot (   ) that all young Koreans have a (   ) idea as to (   ) they want to live in Japanese society.
   (similar, presume, understand, how)

5. (   ) is not something (   ) to you, but something you (   ), develop, and change through (   ) with other people around you.
   (give, identity, create, interact)

UNIT 4 YOUNG KOREANS IN JAPAN

3. Extension

LISTENING CHECK

Listen to a talk and answer the following questions.

1. What is true about "*Zainichi Kankoku-Chōsenjin*"?
    a. They were born in Korea but raised in Japan.
    b. They have never been to Korea.
    c. They are called "Koreans in Japan" in English.
    d. They have the Japanese nationality.

2. What is a "resident card"?
    a. A card issued to Japanese people to go abroad
    b. A card issued to non-Japanese people living in Japan
    c. A card issued to Japanese Americans to get the Japanese citizenship
    d. A card issued to Koreans to travel to Japan

3. According to the speaker, what is the difference between Japanese Americans and Koreans in Japan?
    a. Japanese Americans are the biggest ethnic group in America, but Koreans in Japan aren't.
    b. Japanese Americans can get the citizenship of the country of birth, but Koreans in Japan can't.
    c. Japanese Americans try to hide their ethnicity, but Koreans in Japan don't.
    d. Japanese Americans hold a strong attachment to the country of birth, but Koreans in Japan don't.

4. How is the Korean population changing in Japan?
    a. Shrinking
    b. Growing
    c. Staying the same
    d. Not mentioned

UNIT 5 WHEN SILENCE IS NOT GOLDEN

1. Introduction

BACKGROUND READING

Read the following story and answer the questions below with your partner.

As I started attending a graduate school in the U.S., one thing became very clear to me: American students and Asian students bring different attitudes to the classroom. Since discussion was the major part of the classes in the graduate school, all students were expected to speak up and express their ideas and opinions about the given topic. However, Asian students (including me) seemed unwilling to express their ideas and opinions about what others said. Usually, they didn't even ask a question to the professor or other students. Apparently, this tendency was not related to their English proficiency, as those even very proficient ones were mostly quiet during the class discussions.

As the first semester progressed, there was a department party where all students and faculty members got together. There, I was asked by an American classmate why Asian students are so quiet in the class. I said it's probably because of their cultural background and also the anxiety about speaking English in front of others. She seemed to have understood the anxiety part, but not the cultural part. So, I added a bit more information to what I said; in countries like Japan and Korea, there is a saying "Silence is golden." I also told her that's how we are educated in schools for at least 12 years; the teacher talks and students listen. She seemed a bit surprised but immediately said, "In the U.S., it is believed that discussion is an important part of learning from each other." You are supposed to share your ideas and opinions with other students and even with the teacher. If you don't share your thoughts, it could look like you don't care. So, if you have a chance to study with American students, remember "speaking up does matter with them as it shows you are willing to share and so care."

(P)

UNIT 5 WHEN SILENCE IS NOT GOLDEN

QUESTION

1. What differences did the author notice between American and Asian students in his graduate classes?

2. What reasons did the author give to his colleague about the Asian students' classroom behavior?

3. What student behavior in an American classroom seems to be expected by the teacher and the students?

4. Why does "sharing" mean "caring" in American classrooms?

5. What are typical classroom behaviors expected by the teachers and other students in Japan?

2. Reading Focus

VOCABULARY STUDY

A. Matching: word and meaning

Write the words in the blanks that match their meaning.

| effectively | identify | conduct | priority | distinction |
| conformity | authority | hierarchy | implicitly | participation |

1. _____ : to recognize as being something or someone
2. _____ : the importance you give to something that needs more attention
3. _____ : being similar in form or appearance
4. _____ : the act of differentiating; recognizing of differences
5. _____ : in a way that works well; in effect
6. _____ : to carry out
7. _____ : being part of something
8. _____ : not stated or expressed directly
9. _____ : a system to organize people or things by their ranks
10. _____ : someone or something with power over others

B. Word in Context

Fill in the blanks with the words from the list in Part A. Change the form of the words where necessary.

1. When we _____ an interview, we must be very careful not to ask too personal questions.

2. It is often difficult to _____ Japanese from Chinese or Koreans.

3. Direct eye contact with a teacher is considered a challenge to his _____ in some cultures.

4. Many teachers in my university include _____ in the grading criteria, so I must be actively involved in class activities and discussions.

5. The children's health should be given the highest _____.

6. The politician's speech was so _____ that many people decided to vote for him.

MAIN READING

Read the text below and answer the following questions.

When East Meets West in a Group Discussion

It is a common understanding that in order to work effectively with others, we first need to know each other well. For that, we must meet and talk to each other, and share our views on various issues. It may well be true within the same cultural setting, but when the participants come from different cultural backgrounds, meetings could end up unproductive because of different communication styles that the participants use.

Along the lines of cultural influences on communication styles, researchers have identified a number of different cultural dimensions. Among them, the following three are considered important in relation to how cultural groups conduct their formal discussions:

1. individualistic vs. collectivist
2. high power-distance vs. low power-distance
3. high-context vs. low-context

The first distinction is made between individualistic and collectivist cultures based on what the individual puts the priority on; individual needs or group needs. In the collectivist culture, the group influences most in determining individuals' identity, but in the individualistic culture, personal development comes prior to that of the group. Asian and Latin American countries are categorized under the collectivist culture, while the U.S. and European countries are under the individualistic culture. These collectivist cultures tend to emphasize the importance of conformity and authority as seen in the proverb shared by many Asian countries, "The nail that sticks out is hammered."

Another cultural aspect that influences individuals' communication styles is power-distance: high power-distance and low power-distance. In high power-distance cultures, individuals readily accept the hierarchy within a group and an inequality that arises from it. While East-Asian countries are considered to be relatively high power-distance cultures, New Zealand and the U.S. are viewed as low power-distance societies.

In the high power-distance cultures, leaders are responsible for the conformity and consensus of a group and expected to decide the procedures in discussion. However, in low power-distance cultures, leaders are expected to be democratic and value the participation of individual members in decision-making. For instance, in the U.S., individuals at a meeting may express their ideas and opinions freely without any predetermined order. However, in Japan, individuals may take turns one by one or by appointing the next person after himself. As a sign of passing the turn, they may even use explicit verbal expressions such as "what do you think?" (*dō omoimasuka?*). In a case where there is a senior member of all, he may appoint turns according to the ranks of the participants. One can easily imagine what it is like to have mixed participants from these two different cultures at a meeting.

Finally, the context of communication also influences how individuals conduct their discussions: high- or low-context cultures. In a high-context culture, what is NOT said may be more important than what is said. However, in a low-context culture, individuals' ideas and opinions are important and hence, each member is expected to state his opinions clearly and precisely. In the high-context culture, conflicts are to be avoided in discussion; therefore, opinions are not stated directly and consensus may be reached implicitly or even go unnoticed. For instance, in Japan, no explicit objection may be expressed to others' opinions, so as to save others' face.

In a formal or informal discussion, we first need to be aware that people have different communication styles affected by different cultural values. It is important to be sensitive to both our and others' communication styles for an effective and productive discussion. Such sensitivity is surely the first step to avoid misunderstandings in intercultural meetings.

(P)

UNIT **5** WHEN SILENCE IS NOT GOLDEN

Notes

[6] end up　結局〜になる	[30] responsible for　〜に責任がある, 〜をつかさどる
[8] along the lines of　〜のように, 〜と同様に	[31] consensus　意見の一致, 総意
[9] dimension　次元	[31] procedure　手順, 進行
[10] in relation to　〜と関連して	[35] predetermined order　あらかじめ決められた順番
[12] collectivist　集産主義	[36] take turns　交替でやる
[13] power-distance　権力の格差	[46] precisely　正確に, 的確に
[17] determine　決定する	[49] unnoticed　気づかれない
[19] come prior to　〜に先立つ, 〜より重要である	[52] affect　影響を及ぼす
[23] The nail that sticks out is hammered.　出る杭は打たれる	[53] sensitive　敏感な
[27] inequality　不平等	[54] productive　生産的な, 充実した
[28] relatively　比較的	

READING CHECK

A. Comprehension

Answer the questions based on the reading.

1. What is the main topic of this reading?
    a. The influence of power on social relations
    b. Individual differences in communication styles
    c. Cultural differences between Western and Eastern people
    d. The cultural influences on communication styles

2. According to the reading, which of the following is true?
    a. Brazil belongs to an individualistic culture.
    b. In a collectivist culture, people care more about the individuals than the groups.
    c. There exists a proverb, "The nail that sticks out is hammered." only in Japan.
    d. People in a high power-distance culture are willing to accept the hierarchy in a group.

3. Which of the following countries is mentioned as an example of the collectivist culture?
    a. Japan
    b. European countries
    c. America
    d. New Zealand

4. According to the reading, what does the low power-distance culture value in a meeting?
   a. Structure
   b. Conformity
   c. Democracy
   d. Consensus

5. Which of the following is true about a formal meeting in the low-context culture?
   a. Opposing others' opinion is considered rude.
   b. What is NOT said is more important than what is said in the meeting.
   c. Participants are supposed to listen to others rather than to speak.
   d. Each member's opinions are considered important in decision-making.

B. Key Ideas

Without looking back, complete the sentences with the words in the parentheses. Change the form of the words where necessary.

1. When the participants come from different cultural (   ), meetings could end up (   ) because of (   ) communication (   ) that the participants use.
   (background, different, unproductive, style)

2. In the (   ) culture, the group (   ) most in determining individuals' (   ), but in the individualistic culture, (   ) development comes (   ) to that of the group.
   (identity, personal, prior, collectivist, influence)

3. In the high power-distance cultures, leaders are (   ) for the conformity and (   ) of a group and (   ) to decide the (   ) in discussion.
   (procedure, consensus, expect, responsible)

4. In a (   )-context culture, what is (   ) said may be more important than what is said. However, in a (   )-context culture, (   ) ideas and opinions are (   ).
   (low, important, individuals, high, not)

5. In a formal or informal (   ), we first need to be (   ) that people have different communication styles (   ) by different (   ) values.
   (culture, discussion, affect, aware)

UNIT **5** WHEN SILENCE IS NOT GOLDEN

3. Extension

LISTENING CHECK

Listen to a talk and answer the following questions.

1. What do students do in a group oral exam?
    a. Discuss a topic
    b. Choose a topic
    c. Present a topic
    d. Evaluate other students' speaking

2. How did the speaker feel about the way that his Japanese students conducted the group oral exam?
    a. Interesting
    b. Exciting
    c. Upsetting
    d. Boring

3. Which of the following is true about the speaker?
    a. Not all of his classmates spoke much in his class in the U.S.
    b. He took a group oral exam in his college.
    c. He was often quiet in a group discussion in his college.
    d. He worries too much about others in free discussion.

4. What advice does the speaker give to those who may have a formal meeting with Japanese?
    a. Participate by taking turns.
    b. Show objections to others' opinions.
    c. Don't look at others' faces.
    d. Show a sign that you are listening.

UNIT 6　FLUENT BUT RUDE

1. Introduction

BACKGROUND READING

Read the following story and answer the questions below with your partner.

> A few years ago, when I taught a class at a university in the U.S., there were several students from Japan, who were highly proficient in English and were very eager to learn the topics that I introduced in class. My short break after each class was often taken up by one or two of them who approached me with questions. Every time I met them, they were very polite, and my experiences with them were only to strengthen my stereotype about Japanese students being polite.
>
> Then, I received an email message from one of them that somewhat disappointed me; it's a happening that I still remember even after a decade or more. His message began as a very elaborate explanation of why he had to miss my class, but toward the end, it became rather abrupt and demanding with a saying, "*I want* your handout you gave out in your class." What bothered me with this part of the message was neither the grammar nor the fact that he wanted something from me. It was the expression, "*I want*," which sounded direct and demanding, as if I had no choice but to provide him with a copy of my handout even though it was he who was absent from my class.
>
> Despite still being a learner of English, because he was extremely fluent in English, I was a little upset about him saying, "I want" in his request. I probably took it as rudeness or at least he made me wonder about his real intention by saying, "I want," instead of, "I'd like." As a consequence, that happening still lives in my mind, serving as an example of the impolite use of an English expression by a "highly proficient" Japanese learner of English.
>
> (P)

QUESTION

1. How did the author usually spend short breaks?

2. What was the author's stereotype about Japanese students?

3. Why did the author get upset in the episode?

4. How does the author interpret the use of "I want" by the Japanese student?

5. What behaviors do you think are considered rude in Japan?

2. Reading Focus

VOCABULARY STUDY

A. Matching: word and meaning

Write the words in the blanks that match their meaning.

| behave | convey | deceive | repetitive | otherwise |
| prove | hypothetical | tentative | consequence | impede |

1. _____ : to communicate or make known

2. _____ : doing something again and again

3. _____ : to act properly

4. _____ : based on an idea or theory that seems possible

5. _____ : the result or effect of an earlier happening or action

6. _____ : to disturb; to hinder

7. _____ : not certain or not decided yet

8. _____ : to turn out to be

9. _____ : in a different way

10. _____ : to make someone believe something that is not true; to cheat

B. Word in Context

Fill in the blanks with the words from the list in Part A. Change the form of the words where necessary.

1. Appearances can be _____ — just because something looks good doesn't mean it's good.

2. His decision _____ right.

3. The majority of class liked the new teacher, but he thought _____.

4. This class schedule is still _____ and there's possibility of change.

5. As a _____ of the train delay, I couldn't get on my flight on time.

6. He really doesn't know how to _____ himself.

UNIT **6** FLUENT BUT RUDE

MAIN READING

Read the text below and answer the following questions.

Fluent But Rude

No matter how polite you may behave, if your speech proves otherwise, you become a rude person. In order to get along well with others, how we speak is as important as how we behave. There is an old movie titled, *My Fair Lady* in which a lower-class lady successfully deceives upper-class people about her social class by learning their accents. Although the movie also contained inappropriate messages such as sexism, it conveyed the idea well of how important a role our speech plays in determining how we are perceived by others.

When our English ability has not fully developed yet, our pragmatic errors in speech performance may be considered as a language problem, not as a manner problem. However, as we become fluent, such errors tend to be viewed as signs of rudeness, which will negatively affect our social interactions with others. In other words, pragmatic errors in speech are likely to damage our relationships with other English speakers in intercultural communication.

The good news, however, is while the honorific system of the Japanese language is very complicated, that of English is relatively easy to acquire. By utilizing a few rules, we could sound much more polite in English speech. For instance, adding "please" and "thank you" in your daily conversations will make you sound polite. You can make your "will you ～" request (as in "Will you open the door for me?") even more polite by replacing it with "would you ～." Uses of "will" (or "can") in its past form "would" (or "could") convey the sense of distance from the present reality, thus making your request more hypothetical, indirect, or tentative. By doing so, you are creating a psychological space for your partner to decide on your request. The same principle may apply to an expression like "I was wondering if ～" instead of "I am wondering if ～" and "would you mind ～?" instead of "will you mind ～?"

Another English expression that I find too direct from my students is their frequent use of "no." I understand they go through repetitive training with yes-no questions in English classes, but still they seem too quick to say "no" in their responses. For instance, in deciding the conference schedule, I receive a response like "No, not tomorrow" from my students. However, only by saying, "I'm sorry, but 〜" or "I'm afraid 〜" in the beginning with some reason following, they can make their responses much more polite: "I'm afraid tomorrow is not good because I work part-time on Wednesdays."

You may wonder, "What if we are not sure about the context and how politely we should speak?" Well, it may be a choice of which error you are willing to make: a rude error or a polite error. Who would blame you for being overly polite? However, you can easily imagine what the consequence of the opposite situation would be like.

It may be true that too much worrying about grammar and correct word choice may impede us from speaking English when we are not fluent yet. However, try not to forget that just like Japanese, English is also a language to deliver our feelings, emotions, and intentions. Although it may not be as apparent as Japanese, English also employs different expressions to show different levels of politeness. Whether the purpose of learning English is for a quick overseas trip or for more professional development, wouldn't it be better to leave an image of you behind as a polite person? You never know what an "I would like" could earn you that an "I want" couldn't.

(P)

Notes

[2] no matter how 〜　どれだけ〜しても
[3] rude　失礼な
[3] get along (well) with　つきあう
[5] lower-class　下層階級の
[6] inappropriate　適切でない
[7] sexism　性差別
[12] social interaction　社会における人との関わり
[15] honorific system　敬語体系, 敬語法
[17] utilize　使用する
[24] principle　原理
[28] go through　経験する
[35] What if …?　もし〜だとしたら
[37] overly　過度に
[44] employ　用いる, 採用する

UNIT **6** FLUENT BUT RUDE

READING CHECK

A. Comprehension

Answer the questions based on the reading. (Choose the best answer to complete the sentence.)

1. Speech plays an important role in determining _____.
    a. why we do and don't do certain thing
    b. what we'll do for our living
    c. when we feel like doing something
    d. how we are perceived by others

2. _____ errors in speech performance tend to negatively affect our social interactions with others.
    a. Semantic   b. Syntactic
    c. Phonological   d. Pragmatic

3. The honorific system of the English language is _____ that of Japanese.
    a. not so much complicated as
    b. more problematic than
    c. less complete than
    d. not easier than

4. The author finds "I want ~" and "no" are the examples for too _____ expressions that Japanese students use.
    a. ambiguous   b. repetitive
    c. useful   d. direct

5. _____ that it is better for people to make a polite error rather than a rude error.
    a. It's the fact
    b. It's already proven
    c. The author doubts
    d. The author implies

B. Key Ideas

Without looking back, complete the sentences with the words in the parentheses. Change the form of the words where necessary.

1. There is an old movie (　　), *My Fair Lady* in which a lower-class lady sucessfully (　　) upper-class people about her (　　) class by (　　) their accents.
   (deceive, social, title, learn)

2. When our English ability has not fully (　　) yet, our (　　) errors in speech performance may be (　　) as a language problem, not as a (　　) problem.
   (consider, develop, manner, pragmatic)

3. Uses of "will" in its (　　) form "would" (　　) the (　　) of distance from the (　　) reality, thus making your request more (　　).
   (indirect, present, convey, past, sense)

4. You may (　　), "What (　　) we are not sure about the (　　) how (　　) we should (　　)?"
   (speak, politely, context, wonder, if)

5. Although it may not be as (　　) as Japanese, English also (　　) different (　　) to (　　) different levels of (　　).
   (show, politeness, apparent, employ, expression)

3. Extension

LISTENING CHECK

Listen to a talk and answer the following questions.

1. According to the speaker, which of the following is true?
   a. The Japanese honorific system is most difficult for learners.
   b. Japanese and English have similar honorific systems.
   c. English speakers are ignorant of honorific forms.
   d. Any language has both formal and informal expressions.

2. Why does the speaker talk about his Japanese friend?
   a. To introduce a good English textbook
   b. To show how Americans use formal expression in English

c. To show how difficult it is to be formal or informal in English speech
   d. To explain how enjoyable it is to talk to people at an American party

3. According to the speaker, which of the following is true about his Japanese friend?
   a. She gained a lot of vocabulary by going to parties in the U.S.
   b. She didn't speak English at all before she went to the U.S.
   c. She found it easier to talk to a professor than to a friend at a party.
   d. She wanted to learn how to talk to people at a party.

4. What is the speaker's suggestion about learning different formalities of English?
   a. Join many parties.
   b. Ask close friends.
   c. Try to learn explicitly.
   d. Teach English to students.

UNIT 7 JAPANESE AMERICANS

1. Introduction

BACKGROUND READING

Read the following story and answer the questions below with your partner.

> I have a friend who was born and raised in Chicago, USA. Her nationality is American but her ethnicity is Japanese. I first met her in a class I was taking at a graduate school in the U.S. She was very nice to me and I felt comfortable talking with her, so we soon became good friends. I knew she had some knowledge about the Japanese language, but we never used Japanese when we communicated with each other. Being a native speaker of English, which was the main tool of communication for everybody in the environment at that time, my friend had no reason to speak Japanese with me. I didn't expect her to use Japanese, either, just because she is ethnically Japanese.
>
> Some years later, I had a chance to meet her in Japan. She was in Ōsaka visiting an old friend of hers. For the first time, I saw my friend speaking Japanese (even with some Kansai accent!) very fluently, which surprised me much. Until then, I had had no idea that she was such a good speaker of Japanese. When I asked her why she never told me that she actually speaks Japanese, she said she didn't want people around her to expect that Japanese Americans naturally speak Japanese. I found out that my friend has made a lot of effort studying Japanese since she was in college — she took courses, studied hard for exams, etc. Yet, despite her efforts, people around her took it for granted that she speaks Japanese simply because she is a Japanese American. I remember that she emphasized that Japanese Americans are not "genetically" more advantageous than non-Japanese learners in studying the Japanese language — you need to study the grammar, memorize all *kanji*, and practice the pronunciation, just as other learners of Japanese do. That was the reason why my friend was hesitant to let people (including me) know she is actually a good speaker of Japanese.
>
> (S)

UNIT 7 JAPANESE AMERICANS

QUESTION

1. Why do you think the author's friend first hid the fact that she speaks good Japanese?

2. Why do you think the author's friend decided to study Japanese in the first place?

3. What do you think the author's friend implied by saying "Japanese Americans are not genetically more advantageous than non-Japanese learners"?

4. Do you know anyone around you whose nationality and ethnicity are not the same? If you do, tell your partner about the person's background.

5. Have you ever experienced any situation in which you (intentionally or unintentionally) switched your language, accent, way of talking, or vocabulary? Explain the situation.

2. Reading Focus

VOCABULARY STUDY

A. Matching: word and meaning

Write the words in the blanks that match their meaning.

| laborer | attachment | loyalty | ancestry | courtesy |
| heritage | severe | era | phenomenon | maintain |

1. _____ : the state or quality of being faithful; faithfulness
2. _____ : a family line
3. _____ : politeness; manners
4. _____ : a person who is hired to do physical work
5. _____ : difficult to endure; harsh
6. _____ : an unusual happening, thing, or person
7. _____ : a distinctive period of time in history
8. _____ : to keep something as it is; to preserve
9. _____ : something given by birth
10. _____ : being or feeling tied together; affection

B. Word in Context

Fill in the blanks with the words from the list in Part A. Change the form of the words where necessary.

1. The patient was in a _____ condition.
2. Domestic violence is not a new _____.
3. We are living in an _____ in which information travels so quickly.
4. Mt. Fuji was given World _____ status at a UNESCO meeting in Cambodia.
5. The family could trace their _____ back to the 18th century.
6. I felt a strong _____ to my elementary school.

UNIT 7 JAPANESE AMERICANS

MAIN READING

Read the text below and answer the following questions.

Japanese Americans and Their Language

The first Japanese Americans immigrated to Hawaii in 1868 in order to work as laborers on sugar cane and pineapple plantations. They were called "*Gannenmono*" because it was the first year of the Meiji era. The first generation, or *Issei*, intended to return to Japan after saving a certain amount of money and maintained the language and culture of their homeland. Unlike their expectations, the working conditions at the plantations were very severe: They were forced to work from dawn until dusk under the flaming sun for low wages. Many *Issei* Japanese Americans later found it impossible to save enough money to go back to Japan and ended up staying in the U.S. for the rest of their lives.

Wishing to pass on their linguistic as well as cultural background to their children, or *Nisei*, the first generation Japanese Americans sent their children to Japanese language schools, where they received not only language instruction, but also moral education. Japanese values such as *filial piety, duty, perseverance, courtesy*, and *cooperation* were taught to the second generation there. They were also taught to show the greatest respect for the Japanese emperor and empress. Despite their parents' desire, many *Nisei* children did not succeed in acquiring the Japanese language and culture. To them, Japan was almost like an unknown country to which they had little intention of going and felt little attachment to.

Nisei Japanese Americans went through a very hard time because of discrimination and prejudice in the American society. Many *Nisei* tried to speak only English to prove their loyalty to America especially during World War II. Particularly in Hawaii, after the attack on Pearl Harbor by Japan, the prejudice and discrimination toward the Japanese Americans became worse than ever. This put *Nisei* in a situation where they had to choose between their parents' home country, Japan, and their country of birth, America, which also led to a question about their identity — "Am I Japanese or American?" Whether they wanted to or not, the only way they could survive was to become good American citizens by speaking good English.

The third and fourth generations, on the contrary, were born as "Americans" in an English speaking environment and many of them couldn't speak Japanese at all. Japan was almost entirely a foreign country to them. In this way, the number of Japanese speakers among Japanese Americans decreased as the generation proceeded.

In recent years, however, there has been a phenomenon of language revitalization among young Japanese Americans. Some research shows that about 70% of the students who are taking Japanese classes in Hawaii are of Japanese ancestry. Reasons for studying Japanese may vary — to fulfill the language requirement of schools, to be well-rounded, to make friends, to get better part-time jobs, to better understand the Japanese culture, to maintain their cultural and linguistic heritage, etc. Whatever the reason is, the young Japanese Americans cling to some kind of ties to the country of their ancestors in different ways.

As a Japanese, born and raised, growing up with little knowledge about Japanese Americans, understanding the history and the culture of Japanese Americans provides me with new insights into my native language and culture. Imagining a classroom where little Japanese American *Nisei* children are repeating sentences after their teacher and bowing deeply to the picture of the Japanese emperor gives me very mixed feelings: Were the parents happy about it? Did the children know why they had to do that? At the same time, it makes me stop to think about myself — what it means to be Japanese, to speak Japanese, and live as Japanese.

(S)

UNIT **7** JAPANESE AMERICANS

Notes

[2] immigrate　移住する	[28] the only way　唯一の方法
[3] plantation　農園	[34] proceed　進む
[4] *Gannenmono*　元年者	[36] revitalization　復活
[8] flaming　燃えるように熱い[暑い]	[38] vary　異なる, 一様でない
[11] pass on ~ to …　~を…に引き渡す	[38] fulfill　満たす
[14] filial piety　孝行	[39] requirement　必要条件
[14] perseverance　忍耐	[39] well-rounded　教養のある, 幅の広い
[16] show respect　敬う, 敬意を払う	[42] cling to　握りしめる, 捨てきれない

READING CHECK

A. Comprehension

Answer the questions based on the reading. (Choose the best answer to complete the sentence.)

1. Even after moving to the U.S., the first generation Japanese Americans _____.
    a. learned a new language and culture
    b. rejected a new language and culture
    c. kept their native language and culture
    d. forgot their native language and culture

2. At the Japanese language schools, _____.
    a. Japanese as well as English were taught
    b. Japanese cultural values were emphasized
    c. Japanese was not allowed in the classroom
    d. the teachers were sent from Japan

3. During World War II, _____.
    a. Japanese Americans fought for Japan
    b. *Nisei* Japanese Americans suffered
    c. the population of Japanese Americans increased
    d. more Japanese language schools were opened

4. The third and fourth generation Japanese Americans _____.
    a. generally regarded themselves as Americans
    b. frequently visited Japan

55

c. never experienced prejudice and discrimination
   d. could not find a job without speaking Japanese

5. Which of the following statements would the author agree with?
   a. Japanese people in Japan should know more about the Japanese Americans.
   b. Being a Japanese American is advantageous.
   c. *Nisei* children studying at the language schools were lucky.
   d. The Japanese language has the same significance to all Japanese speaking people.

B. Key Ideas

Without looking back, complete the sentences with the words in the parentheses. Change the form of the words where necessary.

1. The first Japanese Americans (   ) to Hawaii in 1868 in order to work as (   ) on sugar (   ) and pineapple (   ).
   (plantation, immigrate, cane, laborer)

2. (   ) their parents' (   ), many *Nisei* children did not (   ) in (   ) the Japanese language and culture.
   (succeed, desire, acquire, despite)

3. (   ) in Hawaii, after the (   ) on Pearl Harbor by Japan, the (   ) and discrimination toward the Japanese Americans became (   ) than ever.
   (attack, prejudice, particular, bad)

4. Reasons for studying Japanese may (   ) — to fulfill the language (   ) of schools, to get better part-time jobs, to (   ) their cultural and linguistic (   ), etc.
   (requirement, heritage, maintain, vary)

5. (   ) the history and the culture of Japanese Americans (   ) me with new (   ) into my (   ) language and culture.
   (provide, insight, understand, native)

UNIT 7 JAPANESE AMERICANS

3. Extension

LISTENING CHECK

Listen to a talk and answer the following questions.

1. In what part of the mainland U.S. are large communities of Japanese Americans located?
   a. On the East coast
   b. On the West coast
   c. In the Middle East
   d. In the mountain area

2. Who introduced old Japanese terms to Hawaii such as *musubi* and *zōri*?
   a. Local people in Hawaii
   b. Other ethnic groups than Japanese
   c. Japanese tourists
   d. *Issei* Japanese Americans

3. What are you expected to do when you enter somebody's house in Hawaii?
   a. Walk in with your shoes on.
   b. Wear *zōri* inside the house.
   c. Remove your shoes at the entrance.
   d. Pick up your shoes at the entrance.

4. What is the biggest reason for Japanese Americans to cherish Japanese cultural events?
   a. Because children enjoy those events.
   b. Because they can attract tourists.
   c. Because they are an important part of their identity.
   d. Because other ethnic groups hold their own cultural events.

UNIT 8 THE FACE TALKS TOO!

1. Introduction

BACKGROUND READING

Read the following story and answer the questions below with your partner.

A colleague of mine once came to my office with a worried face and asked me if I was upset about what he said in his earlier message. I didn't know what he was saying at first, but soon I realized that he was talking about an incomplete email message that I had sent to him accidently by hitting the send button. This unusually short message of mine made him uneasy and thus, come all the way to talk to me "face to face." We chatted for a while in my office, and upon leaving my office, he said that we all should probably use more face marks (i.e., emoticons) in our text messages so that we can add information about our emotional state to our message. I said, "I agree" and "don't many of us already use emoticons (*emoji*) in our text messages?" Half-jokingly, I also promised I would include an emoticon in the subject line of all my email messages for him.

After my colleague left, I realized I had a professor in my graduate school who used to draw a smiley on students' assignment papers. He never failed to draw one next to the grade he assigned. Honestly, I don't remember what grades I had received from him or even what I learned from his class since a decade has passed since I took his class. However, I will never forget the smiley marks I used to receive from him and still remember how it looked.

Now being a teacher, myself, I also draw a quick smiley on my students' homework papers before I return them. Childish one may think, but trust me: My students love it very much. If you still can't believe me, see below how much more a smiley can speak!

(P)

UNIT **8** THE FACE TALKS TOO!

QUESTION

1. Why did the author's colleague worry?

2. Why did the author's colleague talk about adding a face mark to all email messages?

3. How did the author feel about the smiley mark he used to receive from his professor?

4. Do you agree or disagree with the author about the role of smileys in written communication?

5. Do you use emoticons in your text messages? What are the emoticons you often use? Draw five of them below and ask your partner if he can recognize them. Write down his interpretations in the box below.

	1	2	3	4	5
Your emoticon					
Partner's interpretation					

2. Reading Focus

VOCABULARY STUDY

A. Matching: word and meaning

Write the words in the blanks that match their meaning.

| neglect | component | gaze | equip | detect |
| raise | react | eventually | genuine | aggressive |

1. _____ : to identify or perceive something based on the past experience
2. _____ : to provide someone or something with necessary abilities or materials
3. _____ : honest; sincere
4. _____ : to increase the level or the amount of something
5. _____ : to fail to give enough attention or respect to something
6. _____ : one of the pieces that make up something
7. _____ : after a certain period of time; later
8. _____ : hostile; violent
9. _____ : to look at something for a long time
10. _____ : to act in response to

B. Word in Context

Fill in the blanks with the words from the list in Part A. Change the form of the words where necessary.

1. His _____ behaviors frightened many people in the classroom.
2. Children will _____ become taller than their parents.
3. I don't understand why you had to _____ so negatively to Mr. Tanaka's proposal. I thought it was worth considering.
4. All the politicians at the meeting agreed to _____ the consumption tax.

5. Knowledge, attitude, and skill are the important _____ of intercultural communicative competence.

6. The boy lay on the grass _____ up the sky.

MAIN READING

Read the text below and answer the following questions.

Our Face Is Very Talkative!

No matter how hard we try, misunderstanding seems to occur especially when we communicate through the written channel. Even when we talk on the phone, we often find it difficult to get our meanings across especially in a foreign language. What causes such difficulty? It is the missing nonverbal cues that hinder us from correctly interpreting the speakers' meanings, emotions, and intentions. In addition to body gestures, we use facial expressions to communicate (more efficiently). Consider the reason why many of us use emoticons in our text messages; we wish the reader could correctly interpret our intentions with the support of those facial expressions.

With regard to the role of faces in human communication, scientists argue we are born with a special ability to detect faces. Even before our vision is fully developed, we as babies, begin to gaze at the faces of our caretakers — a sign that face recognition is an important skill for our survival. Eventually, the right brain becomes responsible for face recognition, while the left brain learns to analyze its components, such as eyes, nose, and mouth. From the early life on, we are equipped with the ability for detecting faces and interpreting their expressions, which suggests how important the role facial expressions play in human communication.

Even though face recognition came as Nature's gift, it doesn't mean all people of different cultures use the same expression for the same meaning. Consider the most universal facial expressions, smiling and crying. While undoubtedly all human beings smile and cry, their meanings may differ depending on who does it and where it is done. For instance, while Americans may smile at a stranger saying hello in public places, Japanese would never do so to a stranger in any context. While a Japanese wouldn't cry out loud in a public place, Koreans may do so in a place like a funeral to show how sorrowful they are for their loss. One can easily imagine how a Japanese person would react to a Korean lady crying out loud at a funeral in Japan. As such, the two most fundamental facial expressions could convey different meanings across different cultures.

Another important nonverbal behavior concerns "eye contact" in discussing the role of facial expressions in communication. We all know how important eye contact is in human communication. To mothers, their babies' eye contact is a sure sign of comfort and also normal cognitive development. To adults, tender eye contact and gaze is a sign of growing love, and its avoidance means disinterest. By observing how people make and hold eye contact, we can judge the nature of their relationships.

While eye contact plays an important role in communication, how people do it differs cross-culturally. Americans or Europeans may value direct eye contact as a sign of honesty, interest, and even politeness, whereas Japanese may perceive it as aggressive and rude. Therefore, Americans or Europeans may expect direct eye contact from other participants in a conversation; yet, Japanese participants rather avoid it as a sign of politeness. Likewise, a Korean teacher may consider direct contact by a student as a challenge to his authority, an American teacher may take it as a sign of genuine interest in the conversation. Within the same cultural context, Muslims prefer direct eye contact between people of the same sex, but not between people of the opposite sex, which could confuse non-Muslims even more.

When learning a foreign language, we tend to neglect the nonverbal side of it. As we have seen, communication can be verbal as well as nonverbal. Knowing how important nonverbal behaviors can be in understanding and conducting intercultural communication, wouldn't it be wise not only to learn how to perform verbal behaviors, but also to raise awareness of nonverbal behaviors of our foreign partners?

(P)

UNIT **8** THE FACE TALKS TOO!

> **Notes**
>
> [3] through the written channel 文字を使って
> [4] get one's meanings across 相手に真意を伝える
> [5] nonverbal cues 言葉によらない合図
> [11] with regard to ～については
> [22] universal 万国共通の, 広く行われている
> [22] undoubtedly 疑う余地もなく, 確かに
> [34] cognitive development 認知的発達
> [35] avoidance 逃避, 避けること
> [36] disinterest 無関心
> [44] authority 権威者
> [46] Muslims イスラム教徒

READING CHECK

A. Comprehension

Answer the questions based on the reading. (Choose the best answer to complete the sentence.)

1. What is the main topic of this reading?
    a. How to avoid misreading facial expressions
    b. How to read facial expressions in communication
    c. The importance of face recognition by human beings
    d. The role of facial expressions in communication

2. The author mentions "emoticons" in Paragraph 1 to explain _____.
    a. what "emoticons" are
    b. the importance of facial expressions in communication
    c. how people detect facial expressions
    d. why young people prefer using emoticons in their text messages

3. According to the reading, which of the following is true?
    a. We learn how to smile as we grow up.
    b. Babies begin to gaze at faces after their vision is fully developed.
    c. We use the right brain to read the facial expressions.
    d. People of different cultures may give the different meaning to smiles.

4. According to the reading, what is true of "eye contact" in cross-cultural communication?
    a. Many Koreans consider direct eye contact important.
    b. Many Japanese think direct eye contact is polite.
    c. Many Americans connect direct eye contact with honesty.
    d. Muslim men and women use the same styles of eye contact.

5. Which of the following statements would the author agree with?
   a. It is important to learn about nonverbal behaviors of different cultures.
   b. Facial expressions are more important nonverbal behaviors than body gestures.
   c. It is important not to show your facial expressions in intercultural communication.
   d. Verbal behaviors are more important than nonverbal behaviors in communication.

B. Key Ideas

Without looking back, complete the sentences with the words in the parentheses. Change the form of the words where necessary.

1. (　　) nonverbal cues (　　) us from correctly (　　) the speaker's meanings, emotions, and (　　).
   (interpret, hinder, miss, intention)

2. Even before our (　　) is fully developed, we as (　　), begin to (　　) at the faces of our (　　).
   (gaze, baby, caretaker, vision)

3. Even though face (　　) came as Nature's gift, it doesn't mean all (　　) of different cultures use the same (　　) for the same (　　).
   (meaning, expression, people, recognize)

4. Americans or Europeans may (　　) direct eye contact as a sign of (　　), interest, and even politeness, whereas Japanese may (　　) it as aggressive and (　　).
   (perceive, value, honesty, rude)

5. Wouldn't it be (　　) not only to learn how to (　　) verbal behaviors, but also to (　　) awareness of nonverbal behaviors of our (　　) partners?
   (raise, perform, wise, foreign)

UNIT **8** THE FACE TALKS TOO!

3. Extension

LISTENING CHECK

Listen to a talk and answer the following questions.

1. What did the study that the speaker first mentioned examine?
    a. How people talk to each other
    b. How people express their emotions
    c. How people exchange nonverbal signals
    d. How people understand each other's message

2. According to the speaker, how could we tell if our conversation partner likes us?
    a. By using sign language
    b. By showing different nonverbal signals
    c. By checking if they follow our nonverbal signals
    d. By changing our nonverbal behaviors frequently

3. Which of the following is true about the speakers of different cultures in the talk?
    a. They favored those who used different languages.
    b. They liked those who showed similar body language.
    c. They ignored the body language shown by the others.
    d. They felt comfortable with those who looked similar to them.

4. According to the speaker, what is the lesson we can learn from the studies mentioned?
    a. Nonverbal communication is less important than verbal communication.
    b. We should learn nonverbal behaviors of people from other cultures.
    c. We should use more body language in cross-cultural communication.
    d. Imitation of nonverbal behaviors is easier than learning a foreign language.

UNIT 9 THE V-SIGN WITH CHEESE

1. Introduction

BACKGROUND READING

Read the following story and answer the questions below with your partner.

Having lived in Japan for a few years already, I find myself showing the V-sign when a photo of me is taken with my Japanese friends or students. However, this V-sign shown by most Japanese was a mystery to me for a while, especially because it was often associated with "cheese." I often wondered why Japanese show the V-sign and what it has to do with cheese. I asked several friends around me, but no one seemed to know, which made me do some Google searching.

Apparently it was a topic of discussion without much consensus even on the Web. Also, it was not just me who was wondering about the origin of the V-sign in Japanese photo taking. Nonetheless, here are several reasons that I found from the Internet about why the V-sign got to enjoy its popularity among Japanese:

- Japanese *manga* such as *Kyojin no Hoshi* (巨人の星) or *Sain wa V* (サインはV) popularized the V-sign by which Winston Churchill originally meant "Victory" during World War II,
- The peace sign used by proactive students in the 60's and 70's to show their support for the anti-war movement became increasingly popular in Japan over time, and
- The media popularized the sign by presenting famous figures showing the V-sign in news reports, movies, or TV commercials (especially for a camera company Konica).

However, these ideas still do not answer what the V-sign has to do with cheese. Being a linguist myself, I find the following explanation most plausible: The "cheese" happens to be used because it rhymes well with "peace" and also the [i:] sound makes people look like they are smiling.

No matter what the reason is, why do I also show the V-sign in photos? It's because I'm getting acculturated: I'm learning to behave like Japanese, living in Japan with my Japanese people. Thus, "when in Japan, do as the Japanese do!"

(P)

QUESTION

1. Do you show a V-sign when you take a picture? Why or why not?

2. Up to what age do you think Japanese people generally show a V-sign when taking a picture?

3. Up to what age do you think you will show a V-sign? Why do you think so?

4. Do you know any other culture in which people show a particular sign or say a particular phrase when taking a picture?

5. The author didn't know at first why Japanese show a V-sign when taking a picture. What other things do you think non-Japanese people may wonder about the Japanese customs?

2. Reading Focus

VOCABULARY STUDY

A. Matching: word and meaning

Write the words in the blanks that match their meaning.

| underestimate | caregiver | primitive | subtle | exhibit |
| exaggerate | update | cheat | join | desperately |

1. _____ : to guess that the amount or degree of something is smaller or lower than it actually is

2. _____ : not noticeable or clear

3. _____ : to make something seem larger, more important, or worse than it actually is

4. _____ : belonging to a society at an early stage in the human development

5. _____ : to put two things together

6. _____ : with all of your strength

7. _____ : to make something more modern by adding more or new information

8. _____ : to show clearly or publicly

9. _____ : a person who takes care of a child or an elderly person

10. _____ : to make someone believe something untrue

B. Word in Context

Fill in the blanks with the words from the list in Part A. Change the form of the words where necessary.

1. You are required to provide the name of your _____ on the application form.

2. His paintings _____ his emotional changes.

3. Did you notice the _____ differences between the two pictures?

4. The children _____ hands in a circle.

5. When you have time, would you teach me how to _____ my old computer?

6. The tree has been standing here since the _____ age.

MAIN READING

Read the text below and answer the following questions.

Silent Language

We acquire our mother tongue effortlessly, and likewise we learn most nonverbal behaviors unconsciously. As infants, we imitate and learn to bow by observing how our caregivers greet each other. When we see people say "bye-bye" with a wave of a hand, we quickly learn to wave our hand when we hear someone say "bye-bye." As we grow up, we continuously update our nonverbal behaviors by observing how others conduct theirs to express their meanings, emotions, and intentions. In addition, we learn that the context defines a certain nonverbal behavior appropriate or inappropriate, and all of the nonverbal behaviors suggest certain meanings.

Once we acquire specific nonverbal behaviors, we are no longer conscious about them. It is when we interact with people from different cultures that we realize that the same nonverbal behaviors may convey entirely different meanings and different nonverbal behaviors could suggest the same meaning. For example, the OK sign common in Japan may mean something sexual in a Latin American culture. For greeting, Japanese people bow, Americans shake hands, and Indians say "*Namaste*" by joining their palms together. Just as there exist differences in verbal behaviors, people use different nonverbal behaviors across different cultures.

In its variety, nonverbal communication can be classified into different styles: behavioral and non-linguistic. Behavioral nonverbal communication works through behavioral cues such as body gestures, facial expressions, and physical distance. As a child in Korea, I used to put my arms around my male friend's shoulders walking together. It is not uncommon to find girls walking holding hands in Korea. While these behaviors signal close friendship in Korea, Americans will interpret them entirely differently. While hugging or kissing on the cheek may be a common way of greeting in the U.S., no Japanese would do so to greet their friends in Japan. As For non-linguistic nonverbal communication, people use differing voice volume, pitch, or tone in their speech. After I moved to Japan, I noticed my wife speaking with completely different tones on the phone depending on who was on the other side: a very high tone with someone she's not familiar with and the usual lower tone with her family members.

Communication can be both verbal and nonverbal. Some say we could cheat others with verbal behaviors, but not with nonverbal ones. Nonverbal signs we unconsciously exhibit reveal our true intentions. Considering we carry out 60-70% of our communication through nonverbal behaviors, we can never underestimate the significance of nonverbal behaviors in communication. Furthermore, nonverbal behaviors are known to influence our perception of the speaker's intention much more strongly than verbal behaviors. Indeed, sometimes we can understand our friends better with their gestures, facial expressions, and physical touches than with their words.

Linguists say our spoken language originated from the gestures we used to use in the primitive age; nonverbal behaviors developed much earlier than verbal behaviors. That explains why we desperately show bigger gestures and exaggerated facial expressions when we find it difficult to get our meanings and intentions across with words.

We speak and act based on our cultural norms and values. Nonverbal communication is no exception to this, which makes cross-cultural communication difficult. As nonverbal behaviors are often too subtle to detect, they become the reason for cultural misunderstanding or even conflicts. As so, in our effort to promote cross-cultural understanding, we need to put more conscious effort to better understand how people of different cultures conduct their nonverbal communication. That will certainly help us avoid misunderstandings to occur between our global partners and us.

(P)

UNIT **9** THE V-SIGN WITH CHEESE

Notes

[2] effortlessly　楽に, 努力せずに
[3] nonverbal　言葉を使わない, 言葉によらない
[5] with a wave of a hand　手を振りながら
[17] *Namaste* नमस्ते ((「こんにちは, こんばんは, さようなら」の意のヒンディー語))
[17] palms　てのひら
[21] non-linguistic　非言語的な ((nonverbalより狭義))
[35] carry out　行う
[42] originate from　～から起こる, 生じる
[48] no exception to　～の例外ではない
[51-52] put effort to　努力する

READING CHECK

A. Comprehension

Answer the questions based on the reading. (Choose the best answer to complete the sentence.)

1. Which of the followings do people in general make an effort to learn?
   a. The first language
   b. Foreign language
   c. How to bow
   d. How to wave a hand

2. Once we acquire specific nonverbal behaviors, ＿＿＿＿＿＿.
   a. we usually pay no attention to them
   b. we can interact with anyone from different cultures
   c. we realize that the same nonverbal behaviors may convey different meanings
   d. we realize that different nonverbal behaviors could suggest the same meaning

3. The OK sign is mentioned as an example of nonverbal behavior which ＿＿＿＿＿＿.
   a. has the same meaning in Japan and Latin America
   b. could have different meanings in different cultures
   c. is common in Japan but not in Latin America
   d. we imitate and learn as infants

4. Some say we could cheat others with verbal behaviors, but not with nonverbal ones because ＿＿＿＿＿＿.
   a. there are more variations for nonverbal behaviors
   b. people are more sensitive to verbal behaviors
   c. it is more difficult to hide one's feelings in nonverbal behaviors
   d. it is easier to express our feelings in verbal behaviors

5. According to the passage, which of the following statements is true?
    a. Human beings started using language earlier than gestures.
    b. The author thinks we need more effort to understand our own culture.
    c. Americans do not usually hold hands while walking.
    d. Nonverbal behaviors send more messages in communication than verbal ones.

B. Key Ideas

Without looking back, complete the sentences with the words in the parentheses. Change the form of the words where necessary.

1. As (   ), we (   ) and learn to bow by (   ) how our caregivers (   ) each other.
    (observe, infant, greet, imitate)

2. It is when we (   ) with people from different cultures that we (   ) that the (   ) nonverbal behaviors may (   ) entirely different meanings.
    (realize, convey, same, interact)

3. Behavioral nonverbal communication works (   ) behavioral (   ) such as body gestures, (   ) expressions, and physical (   ).
    (through, distance, facial, cue)

4. (   ) we (   ) out 60-70% of our communication through nonverbal behaviors, we can never (   ) the (   ) of nonverbal behaviors in communication.
    (underestimate, carry, consider, significance)

5. That (   ) why we (   ) show bigger gestures and exaggerated facial expressions when we find it difficult to get our (   ) and intentions (   ) with words.
    (desperately, meaning, explain, across)

UNIT **9** THE V-SIGN WITH CHEESE

3. Extension

LISTENING CHECK

Listen to a talk and answer the following questions.

1. When do Americans move their hand up and down?
    a. When they want to get closer to someone.
    b. When they want to get together with someone.
    c. When they want to keep a distance from someone.
    d. When they want to keep an eye on someone.

2. In the Middle East or South America, why should you not put your thumb up?
    a. Because it may insult others.
    b. Because it would scare others.
    c. Because it is related to money.
    d. Because it looks stupid to others.

3. According to the speaker, which of the following is true about the Muslim culture?
    a. You should not shake hands with others.
    b. You can receive a gift from others with only your right hand.
    c. You must use your left hand for eating.
    d. You often see people making a circle with fingers.

4. According to the speaker, how can you learn different kinds of hand gestures?
    a. By taking classes
    b. By reading textbooks
    c. By asking your teacher
    d. By watching people

73

UNIT 10 WHEN COURTESY FAILS

1. Introduction

BACKGROUND READING

Read the following story and answer the questions below with your partner.

> We all enjoy the feeling of hospitality at a new workplace. Encouraging voices from our new colleagues ease our tension. Welcome remarks from the new senior members help charge up our spirits and leave us full of energy. We can then start off our new career and this entire process happens all together at a ritual called, the Welcome Party.
>
> Right after I moved from the States to teach at my university in Japan, there was again this welcome party, and I was "kindly" requested to be present. Unfortunately though, my tensed spirit was never able to fully relax even after a few toasts and brief chats with a number of people. It was when I bravely decided to become the first one to leave the party that a senior Japanese member of the university approached me. He had this friendly smile on his face and began to talk about how much the university cares about the quality of English education. While to me all of his introductions to the university sounded like just a usual senior's talk, his last words made me so happy: "Please come over to my house someday." I felt I was truly welcomed to be a member of the university family, not just a *gaijin* English teacher. And he added, "We can talk more about these things over Japanese wine (*nihonshu*)," which made me even happier.
>
> Since the welcome party, nine years have passed and I'm still waiting for the opportunity to visit his house for his Japanese wine. As I still see him on campus from time to time, I sometimes wonder if I did anything wrong to make him upset and cancel his invitation. I wonder if I should ask him. Should I?
>
> (P)

UNIT **10** WHEN COURTESY FAILS

QUESTION

1. How does the author describe the welcome party and why does he call it a ritual?

2. What made the author happy at the welcome party?

3. How long has the author been waiting for the invitation?

4. What might have gone wrong with the senior Japanese member's invitation?

5. Should the author ask the senior Japanese member about the invitation? If you were the author, what would you do?

2. Reading Focus

VOCABULARY STUDY

A. Matching: word and meaning

Write the words in the blanks that match their meaning.

| integral | considerate | conceal | endure | integrity |
| embarrass | virtue | negotiation | obvious | inevitable |

1. _____ : showing concerns of others; thoughtful, kind
2. _____ : to keep secret; to hide
3. _____ : the quality of being whole; wholeness; unity
4. _____ : unavoidable
5. _____ : seen or understood easily; apparent
6. _____ : to tolerate; to bear
7. _____ : the quality of being morally good; goodness
8. _____ : a discussion to reach an agreement
9. _____ : essential or necessary
10. _____ : to make someone feel nervous or ashamed in front of other people

B. Word in Context

Fill in the blanks with the words from the list in Part A. Change the form of the words where necessary.

1. The use of audiovisuals was an _____ part of her presentation.
2. The schedule delay seemed _____ considering that there were no trains running due to the heavy rain.
3. It was _____ to me that his relationship was not going well with this girlfriend. They didn't speak a word to each other at the party.
4. Our _____ with the J&J holdings company went well. From the next term, we will research together to produce a new prototype model of our product.

5. Japan has long been concerned about how to achieve the social and political _____ within the country.

6. He has been very _____ toward his colleagues. Whenever they were in trouble, he offered a helping hand without any hesitation.

MAIN READING

Read the text below and answer the following questions.

Know Yourself First in Cross-Cultural Communication

Both living in our home country with foreign nationals and living as a foreign national in a foreign country impose a number of communicative challenges. While many of us think such challenges are due simply to a lack of speaking ability, there are many more fundamental issues involving other aspects of language ability such as cultural knowledge. For instance, no matter how many volumes of Japanese *manga* you go through and no matter how strong your *karate* kicks become, there will always be cultural notions of Japan that you will find difficult to understand as a foreign resident in Japan.

One cultural notion known to be difficult for foreign nationals to understand is the Japanese way of politeness. While the idea that members of a society must be considerate or show respect to others may be universal, it may be realized differently along with different behaviors. For instance, for the same intent of politeness, Americans may tear off the wrapping paper of a gift they've just received as quickly as possible, while Japanese will put much effort into opening it up as nicely as possible. The same intent can be expressed differently by people of different cultures.

One Japanese cultural notion related to politeness is "*honne*" and "*tatemae*": the true feeling (or intention) and the appearances (or faces) presented to others. To those from cultures that value sincerity highly, the Japanese practices of *honne* and *tatemae* may seem unusual. In fact, concealing the true feelings or sometimes even enduring undesirable circumstances (*gaman*) for others has long been a virtue of Japan. To the Japanese people who have valued the integrity and harmony regarded as the ultimate goal for all social systems, "*tatemae*" plays an important role not to embarrass others and hence, not to create conflicts.

We perceive things and interact with others based on the cultural notions that we have internalized since our birth. Likewise, the application of *tatemae* by the Japanese is a subconscious process, which is an integral part of Japanese life. For instance, how *honne* and *tatemae* are handled by Japanese business people at a business meeting once drew attention among western business people who were eager to tie up with a Japanese company. At the negotiation table, the Japanese saying of, "we'll think about your proposal" was sometimes received as a sign of positive endorsement of the deal by western negotiators, while the Japanese counterparts actually meant a "no" to the deal in their politeness.

Why is it difficult to understand others' minds? One obvious reason is because we apply our own cultural values known as "cultural baggage" to the understanding of others' behaviors. People with different cultural backgrounds show different behavioral patterns to the same event, as if seeing the same statue from a different angle. If we wish to truly understand how others' see the statue, it is inevitable to stand first in their position; in other words, be in their shoes.

The idea that knowledge is power has never been truer in this fast changing global society. We should know how our foreign partners approach a given situation, and we need to be aware of how we handle our cultural values. It is probably the latter that is more important in cross-cultural communication because as we expect others to practice their cultural values in consideration of ours, we are expected to do the same by others. Our knowledge of differing socio-cultural values and customs including ours will make not just our life, but also others' much easier in the global society. From where should we start for this mutual understanding? By knowing ourselves, I believe.

(P)

UNIT **10** WHEN COURTESY FAILS

Notes

[2] foreign nationals 外国人, 外国籍の人	[24] the ultimate goal 最終目標
[4] due simply to ~ 単に~が原因で	[27] application 適用, 応用
[7] go through 経験する ((ここでは〈漫画を〉「読む」という意味))	[31] eager to ~しようと熱心な
	[31] tie up with ~と提携する
[13] along with ~と一緒で, ~に加えて	[33] endorsement 承認, 保証
[13] intent 意志	[34] counterpart 相手
[14] tear off 破く, はぎ取る	[40] be in their shoes 彼らの立場に立って
[19] appearance 風貌, 見た目	[45-46] in consideration of ~を考慮して
[20] sincerity 正直さ, 誠実さ	[47] socio-cultural 社会文化的な
[20] practices 習慣	[49] mutual understanding 相互理解

READING CHECK

A. Comprehension

Answer the questions based on the reading. (Choose the best answer to complete the sentence.)

1. What is the main topic of this reading?
    a. Why politeness is important in cross-cultural communication
    b. The importance of knowing oneself in cross-cultural communication
    c. How to be polite in cross-cultural communication
    d. The importance of knowing *honne-tatemae* in Japanese communication

2. According to the reading, which of the following is true?
    a. Being kind to others is not a universal idea.
    b. Many communicative challenges are due simply to a lack of speaking ability.
    c. Tearing off the wrapping paper of a gift is considered impolite in the U.S.
    d. Foreign nationals find it difficult to understand the way Japanese express politeness.

3. The author mentions *honne-tatemae* in the reading to show _____.
    a. the similarity of the ways Japanese and Americans express politeness
    b. how the same idea can be expressed differently according to the culture
    c. why it should not be practiced by Japanese
    d. how difficult it is to understand even by Japanese themselves

4. What does "be in their shoes" mean in Paragraph 5?
    a. Try one's shoes in order to understand him better.

b. To meet someone, clean your shoes first to be polite.

   c. To understand others, see things from their views.

   d. To understand different cultures better, see how people of the cultures wear their shoes.

5. Which of the following statements would the author agree with?

   a. Read as many volumes of *manga* as possible to understand the Japanese culture better.

   b. Be aware both of your and others' culture in cross-cultural communication.

   c. Try to understand other cultures by applying your own cultural values.

   d. Be honest with feelings when you communicate with people from other cultures.

B. Key Ideas

Without looking back, complete the sentences with the words in the parentheses. Change the form of the words where necessary.

1. (   ) challenges involve many more (   ) issues such as (   ) knowledge.
   (fundamental, communicative, culture)

2. One cultural (   ) known to be difficult for (   ) nationals to (   ) is the Japanese way of (   ).
   (understand, notion, foreign, politeness)

3. One (   ) cultural notion related to (   ) is "honne" and "tatemae": the (   ) feeling and the (   ) presented to others.
   (true, appearance, Japanese, politeness)

4. The (   ) of *tatemae* by the Japanese is a (   ) process, which is an (   ) part of Japanese (   ).
   (subconscious, application, life, integral)

5. We should know how our (   ) partners approach a given (   ), and we need to be (   ) of how we (   ) our cultural (   ).
   (situation, foreign, handle, aware, value)

3. Extension

LISTENING CHECK

Listen to a talk and answer the following questions.

1. According to the speaker, which of the following is true?
   a. He took an advanced Japanese class in the U.S.
   b. He took a Japanese class for beginners in the U.S.
   c. He learned Japanese from an American teacher.
   d. He learned Japanese from a boring teacher.

2. Which of the following was not the focus of the Japanese class the speaker took?
   a. Grammar
   b. Conversational expressions
   c. Cultural aspects
   d. Pragmatics

3. Which of the following is true about the speaker?
   a. He was taught not to accept a gift immediately in Japan.
   b. He studied in the U.S. after he got married to a Japanese woman.
   c. He thinks his Japanese class was too difficult.
   d. He has never seen young Japanese saying "*arigato*" when receiving a gift.

4. What is the lesson that the speaker learned from his experience?
   a. We must learn a foreign language only in the classroom.
   b. Learning a foreign language is difficult.
   c. We need to learn how to be polite in a foreign language.
   d. A foreign language must be learned both as knowledge and through experiences.

UNIT 11: TO BECOME A REAL KOREAN

1. Introduction

BACKGROUND READING

Read the following story and answer the questions below with your partner.

> One day, my six-year-old son stunned me at the dinner table by spouting his honest opinion about how he sees Koreans: "Young Koreans are always dancing wildly" [*Wakai Kankokujintte ittsumo odotteru ne!*]. I don't know what led him to reach that conclusion, but my immediate response to him was a question in return: "So, do you see me (his father) 'always' dance?" Soon after a short silence followed his justification: "Well … you are not young and not like other Koreans. You don't live in Korea and you don't speak Korean. Besides, whenever I see 'real' young Koreans on TV, they are 'always' dancing, right?"
>
> Well, he is right at least in his logic. First, to him, I'm only ethnically Korean and cannot be categorized into his "typical" sense of what makes a Korean "Korean." I don't sing; I don't dance; and he hardly hears me speak Korean! Second, my son's primary sources of information about Koreans are mostly TV programs, which show only a limited number of "young" Koreans who come to Japan to perform at a concert or for their promotional events. So, yes, my son is right about his view on young Koreans — they are always dancing whenever he sees them on TV. But even if he is right about his logic, why can't I help but feel uncomfortable with my son's logical thinking of such?
>
> Before I came to Japan, I had had a number of stereotypes about Japan and Japanese people. Living in Japan, I've found that some of them are completely incorrect and others are more or less correct. Now I'm thinking to myself, what if I had never had the opportunity to live in Japan and interact with Japanese folks: My stereotypes would still be just stereotypes.
>
> (P)

UNIT **11** TO BECOME A REAL KOREAN

QUESTION

1. Why do you think the author asked his son if he sees his father dance all the time?

2. What characteristics of Koreans does the son believe to be typical of them? And how are they different from yours?

3. What may be the reason(s) that the author finds his son's way of thinking uncomfortable to accept?

4. What are your images of the following countries and their people?

America	
France	
South Korea	
China	
Brazil	

5. What do you think are the common images about Japan and Japanese people that foreigners may have?

2. Reading Focus

VOCABULARY STUDY

A. Matching: word and meaning

Write the words in the blanks that match their meaning.

| overwhelm | constantly | transmit | composition | trustworthy |
| credibility | generalize | anonymous | dominate | adolescence |

1. _____ : of unknown name
2. _____ : to form a general idea or opinion about a larger group based only on a small number of its members
3. _____ : to send; to pass on
4. _____ : the quality of being trusted
5. _____ : to overcome by power; to overpower with strong forces
6. _____ : makeup; a product of mixing elements
7. _____ : the period of life between the beginning of puberty and adulthood
8. _____ : being considered honest; reliable; dependable
9. _____ : to rule over; to control
10. _____ : without change; continually

B. Word in Context

Fill in the blanks with the words from the list in Part A. Change the form of the words where necessary.

1. We can learn from fossils that the world is _____ changing.

2. Due to the _____ popularity of the City Orchestra, their seasonal tickets are completely sold out already.

3. The researchers are examining the physical _____ of the meteorite that fell onto the city last week.

4. We go through many physical and mental as well as emotional changes during _____ .

5. Dan is very _____ and I can recommend him to you without any reservation.

6. It is dangerous to _____ from only few examples.

MAIN READING

Read the text below and answer the following questions.

Should I Eat Kimchee to Become a Korean?

We all live in a society of overwhelming amounts of information being constantly transmitted in a second. We receive such information sometimes actively and other times passively. We also pass it onto others intentionally or unintentionally. While most of us tend to overly react to our diets that affect our physical compositions; we tend to show too little concern about the quality of information we absorb in our daily lives.

What makes the information from others trustworthy often depends on the credibility of its source. For instance, the value of the stock of a company may rise or fall according to news delivered by NHK, while many of us consider the information from an anonymous website about the company as a hoax.

Another important aspect that determines the trustworthiness of information is related to how appealing it is to our emotional interest. Why are TV commercials dominated by popular entertainers? The same person sometimes comes on multiple advertisements of different products, but we don't really doubt what he says especially if we find him a favorable character. In the end, we tend to see what the commercial producers want us to see.

While these rather harmless TV commercials may satisfy our daily and emotional needs, the ideas and images of individuals, groups of people, or nations that the mass media describe can do much harm to them and also to us. When I was young, I was a big fan of American cowboy movies and used to believe American Indians were brutal aboriginals. Next, I cheered gentle but brave knights when they fought against savage Vikings in European movies. Even before 9/11 occurred, I had feared Middle Easterners as terrorists, thanks to Hollywood action movies. Later in my adolescence, I learned how the western society perceives East-Asians' physical characteristics through *Mulan*, American Indians' through *Pocahontas*, and Hawaiians' through *Lilo&Stitch*, all of which are American animation movies.

We assume many things about others and their cultures. We tend to too hastily generalize our limited knowledge of or experiences with an individual to the society that he belongs to. Once our generalization turns to become a value-laden stereotype, many things that we newly learn come with a surprise. I was surprised to hear from my Japanese friend that he doesn't eat raw fish; and likewise, he first didn't believe me that I don't like kimchee much. All Japanese should love sushi and all Koreans should eat kimchee; that is how we understand the statements, "Sushi is a Japanese dish" and "Kimchee is a Korean dish." While these may be still harmless stereotypes that could affect only your party dishes for your friends of different cultures, negative stereotypes on gender, age, ethnicities, or nations could influence us and our society much negatively. They become bases for prejudice or negative attitudes toward others.

Generalization is an important process of learning about the world, and in the end, no society is free of stereotypes. Yet, we know a statement including, *all*, whether it is literally stated or implied, can be easily falsified by finding a single exception to it. As for stereotypes, we can always try to stand neutral when we hear others' outspoken opinions about sensitive issues before we decide our own side. We know too well how detrimental stereotypes have been on our mutual development in our society; weren't they often the reasons for bullying others and/or their ethnic groups?

(P)

UNIT **11** TO BECOME A REAL KOREAN

Notes

[3] in a second　瞬時に	[29] assume　思い込む, 仮定する
[11] hoax　デマ, 悪ふざけ	[32] value-laden　価値観を含んだ
[16] in the end　結局のところ	[32] stereotype　ステレオタイプ, 固定観念
[20] do harm to　〜に害を及ぼす	[36] statement　主張, 記述
[22] brutal aboriginals　粗暴な先住民	[42] be free of　〜のない, 〜から免れて
[23] savage Vikings　野蛮な北欧の海賊	[43] falsify　論破する, 偽る
[26] *Mulan*　『ムーラン』((1998年公開のディズニーのアニメ映画))	[45] outspoken　無遠慮な, 率直な
[27] *Pocahontas*　『ポカホンタス』((1995年公開のディズニーのアニメ映画))	[45] sensitive issues　デリケートな問題
[27] *Lilo&Stitch*　『リロ・アンド・スティッチ』((2002年公開のディズニーのアニメ映画))	[47] bullying　いじめ

READING CHECK

A. Comprehension

Answer the questions based on the reading.

1. What is the main topic of this reading?
    a. How people learn to trust information from others
    b. What makes people to believe TV commercials
    c. Why generalization is important to understand others better
    d. Importance of understanding and avoiding stereotypes against others

2. What leads people to believe an idea or trust information from others?
    a. Emotional appeals   b. Common sense
    c. Anonymity of the information   d. Entertainers

3. Which of the following is NOT an example of the stereotypes that the author used to have?
    a. American cowboys   b. Vikings in Europe
    c. Middle Easterners   d. Hawaiians' appearance

4. What is the reason that "many things that we newly learn come with a surprise" in Paragraph 5?
    a. Because we realize what we used to know is sometimes wrong
    b. Because we find that there is no exception to stereotypes

c. Because of negative responses from our friends about what we offer

  d. Because of the difference of ideas between others and ourselves

5. Which of the following statements would the author agree with?

  a. It is better to trust information from Internet websites than from NHK.

  b. We must generalize information from limited sources to learn more about others.

  c. We should try to avoid applying stereotypes to understanding other cultures.

  d. When we are not sure about others, we must depend on common stereotypes to judge them.

B. Key Ideas

Without looking back, complete the sentences with the words in the parentheses. Change the form of the words where necessary.

1. What makes the (   ) from others (   ) often depends on the credibility of its (   ) and also how appealing it is to our (   ) interest.
    (trustworthy, emotional, information, source)

2. The (   ) and images of individuals, groups of people, or (   ) that the (   ) describe can do much (   ) to them and also to us.
    (harm, idea, nation, mass media)

3. We (   ) many things about others and their cultures and tend to too hastily (   ) our limited (   ) of or experiences with an individual to the (   ) that he belongs to.
    (knowledge, assume, society, generalize)

4. Negative (   ) on gender, age, ethnicities, or nations could influence us and our society much (   ) and become bases for (   ) or negative (   ) toward others.
    (negative, attitude, prejudice, stereotype)

5. As for (   ), we can always try to stand (   ) when we hear others' (   ) opinions about (   ) issues before we decide our own side.
    (sensitive, neutral, stereotype, outspoken)

UNIT **11** TO BECOME A REAL KOREAN

3. Extension

LISTENING CHECK

Listen to a talk and answer the following questions.

1. According to the speaker, how are people in Hawaii sometimes described?
    a. As hula dancers
    b. As surfers
    c. Lazy
    d. Being rude to tourists

2. Which of the following serves as a commercial stereotype for Hawaii?
    a. Aloha
    b. O'Hana
    c. Pidgin English
    d. Hula dancers

3. Which of the following is true, according to the talk?
    a. All stereotypes about Hawaii are wrong.
    b. There are negative stereotypes about Hawaiian people.
    c. The speaker thought only rich Japanese visited Hawaii.
    d. The speaker later found out that his stereotypes about Japanese were all wrong.

4. What is the stereotype that the speaker currently holds about Japanese?
    a. They show a V-sign when taking a photo.
    b. They are rich.
    c. They always carry an expensive bag.
    d. They are all photographers.

UNIT 12 DOES AGE MATTER?

1. Introduction

BACKGROUND READING

Read the following story and answer the questions below with your partner.

>It was a few years ago in Seoul, Korea when I saw an elderly Korean man having an argument with a young foreign man on a subway platform. I was in a hurry running down the stairs to find my train, but such a loud, angry voice in a public place was not something that I, and probably others, too could ignore easily. It drew my attention especially because it was a Caucasian, most likely an American considering his English accent, whom the Korean man was having an argument with. I slowed down my pace to find out what was going on as I was passing them.
>
>I don't know how long the argument went on after I left; my train arrived before long, and I left the scene immediately. However, two things were clear to me: First, the Korean man was able to understand and probably speak at least some English, and second, the American didn't understand why the old Korean gentleman was yelling at him. The Korean man was yelling at him both in Korean and in English — "How old are you?" and "You call me YOU?", and the young American was just repeatedly saying, "What did I do wrong?" I do not know what and who started the argument to begin with, but apparently the *old* Korean man got (even more) upset because he was referred to as "YOU" by the *young* American.
>
>So, what was really the problem with the old Korean man? Why did the expression "YOU" matter to him so much? I know Koreans care much about age, as depending on that, they'll have to use different honorific forms. However, I wonder if it was right at all that the old Korean man demanded the same linguistic politeness from a foreign national in Korea.
>
> (P)

UNIT **12** DOES AGE MATTER?

QUESTION

1. What do you think caused the argument between the Korean and the American persons in the situation?

2. Why do you think it mattered to the Korean person that he was referred to as "YOU" in the conversation?

3. How would you feel if you were the American person?

4. Have you seen any Japanese being involved in an argument with a foreigner in Japan? What was the reason for the argument?

5. How does age matter to you when communicating with others (Japanese and foreigners)?

2. Reading Focus

VOCABULARY STUDY

A. Matching: word and meaning

Write the words in the blanks that match their meaning.

| governor | uneasy | proper | considerable | upbringing |
| unity | constant | secure | bother | philosophy |

1. _____ : correct in behavior; appropriate or suitable
2. _____ : the state or quality of being one
3. _____ : a set of beliefs and ideas about what is important in life
4. _____ : large in number, amount, or degree; a lot or much
5. _____ : continuous; persistent
6. _____ : a person who is the leader of a particular area
7. _____ : to obtain or save; to keep safe
8. _____ : the way a child is raised
9. _____ : to disturb; to cause trouble to
10. _____ : anxious; uncomfortable

B. Word in Context

Fill in the blanks with the words from the list in Part A. Change the form of the words where necessary.

1. His father was elected as a _____ of the prefecture.
2. To build the new city library, a _____ amount of tax money will be spent.
3. I was _____ interrupted by my neighbor's dog last night and couldn't sleep well.
4. Various experiences will help you develop a _____ of life.
5. I feel _____ whenever people ask me where I'm from.

6. Residents in the neighboring towns have _____ to show their strong opposition to the city's plan to build a new apartment complex for city workers.

MAIN READING

Read the text below and answer the following questions.

Confucianism and English: Why don't they get along?

For any intercultural communication to be productive, we first need to recognize the cultural values that the people bring in their conversations. Only after we understand their cultural values, can we correctly interpret the meanings and intentions of the speech that is delivered to us. How can we increase our understanding of different cultural values? One way may be to consider how the history has helped the society to shape its traditional values.

Consider the case of the three East Asian countries, China, Japan, and Korea. While people from these countries look similar in their appearances, there are a number of differences in their value systems. A case in point is they all eat rice, with different utensils in different eating manners: Chinese use long chopsticks, Japanese use shorter ones and they both hold their rice bowl closer to their mouth; whereas, Koreans use both a spoon and chopsticks, but leave their rice and soup bowls on the table. We can easily imagine how people of these three countries would feel about each other if they eat together. We don't just see each other's eating behaviors, but rather interpret and judge them with our own value system.

Another "similar but different" example can be found from the political philosophy of these three countries — Confucianism. Confucianism is a philosophy for proper human relationships, which has played a considerable role in forming the traditional values of these countries. While the original form was similar, Confucianism has taken different paths for survival in responding to different political and social changes in these countries. Chinese may say "One (一)" as the most important social principle, while Japanese, "Harmony (和)" and Koreans, "Loyalty (忠)." China, a nation of vast territory and small kingdoms, had to emphasize the importance of unity, so as to manage the entire nation without conflicts. You may have heard the expression, "One China" policy. Japan, an island country, had tried to avoid all possible internal conflicts as they could lead the people to nowhere but to the sea. Therefore, harmony and peace had to be kept more than anything else. Finally, to people in Korea, a country with constant invasions by its neighboring countries, showing "loyalty" to the governors was an important way to secure future protection.

In defining social relations in China, Japan, and Korea, the language also played an essential role; the three languages all include their own honorific forms. By showing your status compared to the person you are talking to, honorifics can convey your sense of respect to him, which is very important in Confucianism. However, when we have to speak a foreign language that does not utilize an explicit honorific system, we easily feel uncomfortable. For instance, no matter how well you speak English, you may still find it difficult to deliver your sense of politeness without specific honorific forms.

I was educated in the U.S. and have taught English for a long time. However, I still feel uneasy when I speak English to my senior Koreans or Japanese superiors. I must say what bothers me the most in English is the pronoun "YOU." When I call them "YOU," I feel I'm not properly positioning myself against them to show my respect. I wonder what has happened to all the education and life support I have received in the U.S. and Japan, because my background of such seems still too weak to beat my Confucian upbringing. On one hand, now I can eat rice with chopsticks like Japanese or Chinese, or with a spoon like Koreans, or even a fork. When it comes to politeness, however, I just cannot turn off my switch of this Confucian background easily.

(P)

UNIT **12** DOES AGE MATTER?

Notes	
[1] Confucianism　儒教	[34] honorific　敬語の; 敬語
[3] bring　〈価値などを〉取り入れる	[42] superior　目上の人
[10] value systems　価値基準	[44] position oneself　立場をわきまえる
[10] a case in point　適例, 好例	[47] Confucian　儒教の
[11] chopsticks　箸	

READING CHECK

A. Comprehension

Answer the questions based on the reading. (Choose the best answer to complete the sentence.)

1. What is the main topic of this reading?
    a. The role of the traditional values in intercultural communication
    b. The influence of Confucianism on the societies of China, Japan, and Korea
    c. The differences among Chinese, Japanese, and Koreans in their value systems
    d. The similarities of the traditional values of China, Japan, and Korea

2. For any communication to be productive, people must _____.
    a. recognize different cultural values   b. ignore each other's differences
    c. avoid expressing their opinions   d. find similarities of each other

3. _____ has had a deep impact on political ideology in East Asian countries.
    a. Buddhism   b. Confucianism
    c. Christianity   d. Nationalism

4. It may be difficult for Koreans to _____.
    a. explain the use of "YOU" in Korean to foreigners
    b. attach a honorific sense to their English speech
    c. use Korean pronouns to their superiors
    d. learn English honorific expressions

5. The author feels uncomfortable when he has to _____.
    a. speak English to Americans
    b. behave based on his Korean values
    c. convey his respect to Korean superiors
    d. call his superiors "YOU" in English

95

B. Key Ideas

Without looking back, complete the sentences with the words in the parentheses. Change the form of the words where necessary.

1. For any (   ) communication to be (   ), we first need to (   ) the cultural (   ) that the people bring in their conversations.

    (recognize, intercultural, value, productive)

2. We don't just (   ) each other's eating (   ), but rather interpret and (   ) them with our own (   ) system.

    (judge, value, behavior, see)

3. (   ) is a philosophy for proper human (   ), which has played a (   ) role in (   ) the (   ) values of China, Japan, and Korea.

    (relationship, form, Confucianism, traditional, considerable)

4. (   ) has taken different (   ) for survival in (   ) to different (   ) and social changes in Asian countries.

    (respond, Confucianism, political, path)

5. In (   ) social relations in China, Japan, and Korea, the (   ) also played an (   ) role; the three languages all include their own (   ) forms.

    (essential, honorific, language, define)

3. Extension

LISTENING CHECK

Listen to a talk and answer the following questions.

1. According to the speaker, what was difficult for him in the U.S.?
    a. To hold a status of high respect
    b. To teach the Korean culture in school
    c. To change his nationality
    d. To put aside his Korean values

2. What does the Korean saying "One should not step even on the shadow of his teacher" mean?
    a. Students should not walk behind their teachers.

b. Students should climb up stairs ahead of their teachers.

   c. Teachers should teach students how to avoid shadows.

   d. Students should respect their teachers.

3. According to the speaker, which of the following can be implied?

   a. He lived in the U.S. when he was little.

   b. In Korea, teachers are not respected by their students.

   c. Korean language has honorific forms.

   d. He doesn't need to show respect to the elderly in English.

4. What is the problem with the speaker?

   a. He knows little about English pronouns.

   b. He doesn't like to be called "YOU" by his teachers.

   c. He feels uncomfortable to call his teacher "YOU."

   d. He doesn't like the way that other Koreans call him.

UNIT 13 GREAT WAIT

1. Introduction

BACKGROUND READING

Read the following story and answer the questions below with your partner.

It was more than twenty years ago when I first went to the U.S. for my graduate study. I visited the school with a letter in my hand from the graduate school, inviting me to a department orientation for incoming students. I expected that all of the detailed information would be provided at the orientation, so I waited eagerly for the occasion.

Despite my expectations, the orientation appeared extremely informal primarily because it was held in someone's house with only less than twenty people. (Later, I learned that the school actually owned the house.) What surprised me most was that no specific information was explained at the orientation. All I remember now is that a director from the school talked and everyone introduced themselves briefly. That was it. I left the place, hoping that somebody from the graduate office would feed me the information. I waited and waited, but I didn't hear from anyone.

Two days before the quarter was to begin, I finally decided to consult with the director of the graduate school. When I visited his office, the door was already open. He was casually dressed and looked friendly with a smile on his face. I was desperate to know how to register for my classes. I didn't even know how to start taking a class. He was patient enough to explain about the registration process and gave me some advice about classes that I should take. I thanked him and left his office. On my way home, I stopped by an administration building for class registration, and it didn't take very long until I was all set for the first day of my first class in the U.S. I still remember all of the uncertainty and anxiety I had gone through on that particular day.

(K)

UNIT **13** GREAT WAIT

QUESTION

1. What kind of meeting did the author think the orientation would be like?

2. Why did the author decide to visit the director of his school?

3. Do you want to study abroad someday? Where? Why?

4. Have you ever been abroad for study? If so, where?

5. What would you do in order not to experience a similar incident as the author's?

2. Reading Focus

VOCABULARY STUDY

A. Matching: word and meaning

Write the words in the blanks that match their meaning.

| orientation | theory | episode | improve | examine |
| consultation | submit | expose | treat | prevail |

1. _____ : a formal idea or a set of ideas to explain something systematically
2. _____ : to make things better
3. _____ : a meeting for advice
4. _____ : to deal with; to handle
5. _____ : to look carefully into something; to inspect
6. _____ : to become common or accepted as common by people
7. _____ : to hand in; to turn in
8. _____ : one of a series of events
9. _____ : to give someone a chance to experience a new idea or activity
10. _____ : the attitude of a person or the position of a thing related to a particular idea or situation

B. Word in Context

Fill in the blanks with the words from the list in Part A. Change the form of the words where necessary.

1. I need to _____ your left eye first, so please try to keep it open.
2. Haven't you _____ your scholarship application yet? You know the deadline is tomorrow, right?
3. Parents tend to _____ boys and girls differently when they are still young.
4. What was the last _____ of the show about? I forgot to ask you to record it for me.

5. If you really want to _____ your English speaking, you must not be afraid of making errors in your speech.

6. NASA recently announced that they now have a new major _____ that can explain the origins of life.

MAIN READING

Read the text below and answer the following questions.

Critical Incident

Intercultural Communication, or Cross-Cultural Communication, is the study of communication between people from different cultures. It looks at their communicative practices and behaviors, and especially the problems that may arise when they interact with each other. Intercultural Communication has been in existence for a little over half a century, with its origins right after World War II. As a scholarly field, Intercultural Communication has a multi-disciplinary orientation, drawing on a number of theories, practices and research methods from other scholarly fields that have already been popular in the Social Sciences.

In training students with Cross-Cultural Communication, a number of techniques have been employed and one of them is "Critical Incident." Critical Incident means an event which bears a significant meaning to an individual. The incident I introduced in the background reading was "critical" to me because it provided me with a precious opportunity to recognize a significant difference between Japan and the U.S. at the start of my life as a graduate student. This method of "Critical Incident" has been widely used in intercultural training as a technique to understand other people's experiences through their eyes and voices. If someone experiences different cultures overseas, for example, he can introduce that experience in the form of an episode. Then, the episode can be discussed and shared in groups to learn what it means to be exposed to intercultural differences. These procedures of Critical Incident are often employed by both trainers and trainees to improve their ability to make isomorphic attribution. Isomorphic attribution is an idea that in order for someone to understand others' behavior in a different culture, he should examine the behavior in light of his own cultural background.

The episode in the previous reading is what I actually experienced in the U.S. when I went there for my graduate study. To my surprise, after a few years of study in human communication, I learned that there is a method called "Critical Incident" used in intercultural training and one such episode is called the "Great Wait." The situation of the episode is a bit different than mine, but both episodes go parallel in terms of the lesson to be learned by intercultural trainees.

The lesson that I learned through the incident is the importance of taking initiative. As a graduate student, you need to take initiative to ask for consultation. Asking questions, getting advice, and submitting proposals, all these actions you need to do first before you call on your academic advisor. In Japan, it is the norm that the higher ranking person, like an academic advisor in a university, comes to you by taking the initiative and subordinates wait for them to approach on an occasion when asking for consultation. Interpreting what's happening in the U.S. based solely on my own experiences in Japan, I expected someone from the graduate school to give me advice instead of me having to take the initiative. That's not how things work in the U.S. No matter what status you may have, students should be treated equally as their academic advisors and even international students must take the initiative to get help.

Nowadays, more and more schools in many countries have become interculturally sensitive and some schools may provide an international-student-friendly learning environment. Still, graduate students are expected to act according to the norms that prevail in the society; thus, they may encounter situations considered to be a critical incident even on a seemingly globalized university campus.

(K)

UNIT **13** GREAT WAIT

Notes

[1] Critical Incident　クリティカル・インシデント，危機的事例
[5-6] be in existence　存在する
[7] scholarly field　学究的な分野
[7] multi-disciplinary　学際的な
[8] draw on　参考にする
[8] research methods　調査方法
[9] Social Science　社会科学
[23] isomorphic attribution　同型帰属
[25] in light of　～に照らして，～の観点から
[31] go parallel　同等である
[31] in terms of　～という点で，～に関して
[32-33] take initiative　イニシアチブをとる
[35] call on　～を訪問する
[37] subordinate　部下
[46] -friendly　～にやさしい，～に使いやすい
[48] seemingly　見たところは，表面上は

READING CHECK

A. Comprehension

Answer the questions based on the reading. (Choose the best answer to complete the sentence.)

1. Intercultural Communication is a study about what communicative processes people from different cultures experience when they _____.
    a. exchange business cards　　　b. watch TV and movies
    c. interact with each other　　　d. communicate online

2. In intercultural training, trainees can learn _____ with critical incident.
    a. the importance of debate through many exercises
    b. other people's experiences through their eyes and voices
    c. how to protect their families in the event of catastrophe
    d. by heart both basic and advanced arithmetical formulas

3. Which of the following does the author NOT mention as an example of taking initiative?
    a. Asking questions　　　b. Getting advice
    c. Visiting an advisor　　　d. Submitting proposals

4. The author learned the importance of taking initiative mainly through _____.
    a. his own experience　　　b. his friend's experience
    c. his high school teachers　　　d. intercultural training

5. The author thinks fewer problems exist for the current international students because more and more schools have become _____.

a. internationally famous
b. interculturally sensitive
c. intellectually capable
d. interactively competent

B. Key Ideas

Without looking back, complete the sentences with the words in the parentheses. Change the form of the words where necessary.

1. Intercultural Communication has a (　　) orientation, (　　) on a number of (　　), practices and research methods from other (　　) fields.
    (draw, scholarly, multi-disciplinary, theory)

2. The (　　) of "Critical Incident" has been widely (　　) in intercultural training as a technique to (　　) other people's experiences through their eyes and (　　).
    (use, understand, method, voice)

3. Isomorphic (　　) is an idea that in order for someone to understand others' behavior in a (　　) culture, he should (　　) the behavior in light of his own cultural (　　).
    (examine, different, attribution, background)

4. The (　　) that I learned (　　) the incident is the (　　) of (　　) initiative.
    (take, through, importance, lesson)

5. Nowadays, more and more schools in many (　　) have become (　　) sensitive and some schools may (　　) an international-student-friendly (　　) environment.
    (provide, learn, country, intercultural)

3. Extension

LISTENING CHECK

Listen to a talk and answer the following questions.

1. According to the speaker, for what reasons has the number of Japanese students studying in the U.S. decreased?
    a. Educational and religious reasons
    b. Safety and economic reasons
    c. Philosophical and social reasons
    d. Personal and political reasons

2. In what countries, has the number of international students to the U.S. decreased?
    a. All the countries

b. Japan, China and Saudi Arabia

   c. All the countries except China and Saudi Arabia

   d. Only Japan

3. Which of the following does the speaker mention as a disadvantage of online courses?

   a. High cost

   b. Digital device

   c. Little consideration for the environment

   d. Nothing in particular

4. According to the speaker, which of the following is true?

   a. MIT lost international students due to online courses.

   b. Online lectures motivate students to study on-site.

   c. Only very limited scholarships are available for online courses.

   d. The application process takes longer for web registration.

UNIT 14: DIALOGUE IN AN AGE OF CONFLICT

1. Introduction

BACKGROUND READING

Read the following story and answer the questions below with your partner.

It seems such a long time ago when Japanese people were obsessed with the Korean drama "Winter Sonata." Many people showed an addictive behavior toward the TV program and quite a few kept watching the same episode over and over again until the break of dawn. Some fans turned out to be like paparazzi and even fell in love with the main character. It seems just as long ago when *1wave after wave of K-Pop hit the Japanese music scene until it reached a level in which the older generations were no longer able to tell them apart from the music bands originally from Japan. Thanks to the Korean cultural boom in Japan, South Korean and Japanese people were able to bridge the cultural gap and feel closer to each other for the first time in many decades.

Now that the popularity has died down, protest rallies against Korean communities are in the headlines of the daily news. Shin-Ōkubo, Tokyo, boasting of itself as the largest Korean town in Japan, *2is now shadowed with placards painted with slogans like, "I hate Koreans!" and "Go to hell." Even the Japanese Prime Minister touched on the topic of the demonstrations in one of the government committees, trying to discourage anti-Korean groups from engaging in *3hate speech activities.

Where did this abrupt change in people's attitudes come from? How could we have foreseen these changes and how could we have prevented them? Unfortunately, the mechanisms of hate speech are yet unknown, but the things we are sure of are twofold: First, nobody knows who will be the next target of these hate speeches. Second, no one wants to be the next target. I'm sure it's certainly not you.

(K)

*1 wave after wave of 次々と押し寄せる〜
*2 be shadowed with 〜で覆われる
*3 hate speech ヘイトスピーチ, 憎悪表現

UNIT **14** DIALOGUE IN AN AGE OF CONFLICT

QUESTION

1. Why do you think Japanese people have been attracted to South Korean culture?

2. What do you think caused the hate speech against Korean people?

3. How would you feel if you were the Korean person who was the target of the cultural boom and later hate speech?

4. What do you think about freedom of speech? Should it be protected even if it might hurt other people's feelings?

5. How cautious are you about what you say so as not to hurt other's feelings?

2. Reading Focus

VOCABULARY STUDY

A. Matching: word and meaning

Write the words in the blanks that match their meaning.

| resolve | abduct | stance | diplomatic | territorial |
| criticism | contradictory | plural | simultaneously | contribute |

1. _____ : the position where a person stands
2. _____ : of or relating to a land
3. _____ : an unfavorable comment; attack
4. _____ : not consistent; being opposite to each other in meaning
5. _____ : to find a solution to something
6. _____ : to carry off someone illegally; to kidnap
7. _____ : to be an essential part of something and help it to be successful
8. _____ : happening at the same time
9. _____ : composed of more than one
10. _____ : of or relating to diplomacy

B. Word in Context

Fill in the blanks with the words from the list in Part A. Change the form of the words where necessary.

1. The writer was not happy to read _____ about the novel he has just published.
2. The politician never made his _____ clear on the issue of nuclear plants.
3. We wouldn't have been able to achieve our goal without your great _____.
4. Recent relationships between China/Korea and Japan have become worse due to the _____ conflicts.
5. The committee has been working diligently to _____ the tension between the employer of the company and his employees.

6. We are not programmed to do different tasks _____. We are supposed to perform a task one by one.

MAIN READING

Read the text below and answer the following questions.

Dialogue

When governments are confronted with diplomatic issues, they frequently refer to "dialogue" to make it clear where they position themselves in the process of resolving such conflict. This brings to mind recent developments in the release of abducted victims in North Korea. The former Prime Minister Noda with the Democratic Party of Japan used "dialogue" to try to set the stage where North Korea and Japan could start discussing the issue. Unfortunately, the Noda administration was dissolved too soon and was not able to even start the discussion on how his government would have approached the issue.

After the landslide victory by the Liberal Democratic Party, Prime Minister Abe decided to take a more hawkish stance toward the issue. He has the belief that dialogue only, is not enough to resolve the problems, but dialogue and conflict (*tairitsu*) can. As you may know, Prime Minister Abe had significantly contributed to the release of abducted victims in North Korea a decade ago by means of giving the North diplomatic pressure.

Japan has continuously had conflicts with its neighboring countries; territorial issues with China and Korea have remained as the most critical ones that need immediate actions. It appears that no matter how hard the governments try, there seems to be no easy solutions to ease the tensions between the three countries. In such cases, all that the politicians can say is that the door to dialogue remains open. But no one seems to be actually willing to enter into or capable of entering into the room; it is as if the door opening was too narrow to squeeze into.

On the scholarly side, Mikhail Mikhailovich Bakhtin, a Russian scholar of literary criticism, is the most widely known dialogist whose ideas are centered on a notion of dialogue. Many scholars in a variety of fields including literary criticism, linguistics, communication studies, education, and language acquisition have employed Bakhtin's idea.

Bakhtin suggested the concept of "multi-vocality" to characterize Dostoyevsky's novels. Instead of different characters addressing and responding with each other through an author's monologue, Dostoyevsky's characters independently engage in addressing and responding with each other, thus creating spaces where plural and sometimes contradictory voices are coexisting. Characters can act independently from the intent of the author's monologue, and the spaces are filled with a number of characters' voices and the author's voice.

Communication studies borrow his idea of dialogue to address a weakness of the traditional one-way linear communication model that had been the most influential of all in the field. Multi-vocality supports the idea that more than one voice simultaneously addresses and responds with each other, thus diminishing the nature of one-way and linear interactions between the two communication participants.

Scholars interested in intercultural communication have resorted to intercultural dialogue after having learned failures of acculturation and multi-cultural coexistence in the European Union. Acculturation worked as a policy by which a host culture monologically imprinted their culture onto a group of newly immigrated people. Meanwhile, multi-cultural coexistence allowed ethnic groups to live in their own respective cultures; whereas, they came to be left alone with minimum communication with the host society. Ethnic communities ended up isolating each other. Thus, by using the concept of multi-vocality, the EU has been trying to unite these isolated communities to collaborate with each other, even if they possess different cultural backgrounds.

Likewise, theories and practices of dialogue are rampant. It suggests that dialogue can provide us with epistemological, ontological, and pragmatic means to understand what it means for humans to communicate.

(K)

UNIT **14** DIALOGUE IN AN AGE OF CONFLICT

Notes

[2] be confronted with 　～と直面する
[3] refer to 　～に言及する
[4] bring to mind 　思い起こさせる
[5] release of abducted victims 　拉致被害者の解放
[6] the Democratic Party of Japan 　民主党
[6] set the stage 　場を設ける，お膳立てをする
[8] administration 　内閣，陣営
[8] be dissolved 　解散させられる
[10] the landslide victory 　圧勝
[10] the Liberal Democratic Party 　自由民主党，自民党
[11] take a more hawkish stance 　さらにタカ派的な姿勢をとる
[14-15] by means of 　～によって，～という手段を用いて
[19] solution 　解決策
[19] ease the tension 　緊張を和らげる
[22] squeeze into 　割り込む，すべり込む
[23] Mikhail Mikhailovich Bakhtin 　ミハイル・ミハイロビッチ・バフチン (1895-1975)((ロシアの文芸批評家))
[24] literary criticism 　文芸批評
[24] dialogist 　対話者，対話劇作者
[26-27] language acquisition 　言語習得
[28] multi-vocality 　多声性
[29] Dostoyevsky 　ドストエフスキー (1821-81)((ロシアの小説家))
[30] monologue 　モノローグ
[39] diminish 　弱くする，衰えさせる
[42] resort to 　～を最後の手段にする
[43] acculturation 　文化的適応，文化変容
[43-44] multi-cultural coexistence 　多文化共生
[45] monologically 　独断で，独白的に
[45] imprint 　刻み込ませる
[47] come to 　～するようになる
[49] isolate 　切り離す，隔離する
[52] rampant 　蔓延した
[53] epistemological 　観念論的な
[53] ontological 　存在論的な
[53] pragmatic 　実用主義的な

READING CHECK

A. Comprehension

Answer the questions based on the reading. (Choose the best answer to complete the sentence.)

1. What is the main topic of this reading?
    a. The role of dialogue in the fields of politics and communication
    b. The contribution of Mikhail Mikhailovic Bakhtin to the development of politics
    c. Why multi-vocality is important in understanding human communication
    d. How to resolve conflict through dialogues

2. What political belief does Prime Minister Abe have toward the North Korea?
    a. Dialogue can easily solve the problem.
    b. Dialogue is no use in solving the issue.

c. Dialogue and conflict can work out the issue.

  d. Indirect dialogue will bring the world a peace.

3. Communication studies borrow Bakhtin's idea of dialogue to _____ the traditional one-way linear communication model that had been the most influential of all in the field.
   a. support the importance of
   b. address a weakness of
   c. deny a possibility of
   d. newly create

4. EU came to a conclusion that _____ cannot resolve regional conflicts within EU.
   a. multi-vocality
   b. acculturation
   c. dialogue
   d. globalization

5. Dialogue is a meaningful way to _____.
   a. understand human communication
   b. give meaning to philosophy
   c. boost up the Japanese economy
   d. improve your linguistic aptitude

B. Key Ideas

Without looking back, complete the sentences with the words in the parentheses. Change the form of the words where necessary.

1. When governments are (   ) with diplomatic issues, they (   ) refer to "dialogue" to make it clear where they (   ) themselves in the process of (   ) such conflict.
     (confront, resolve, position, frequent)

2. After the (   ) victory by the Liberal Democratic Party, Prime Minister Abe decided to (   ) a more hawkish (   ) toward the (   ).
     (take, stance, landslide, issue)

3. It appears that no (   ) how hard the governments try, there (   ) to be no easy solutions to (   ) the tensions between the three (   ).
     (seem, ease, matter, country)

4. (   ) worked as a policy by which a (   ) culture monologically (   ) their culture onto a group of (   ) immigrated people.
     (imprint, newly, acculturation, host)

5. By (   ) the concept of multi-vocality, the EU has been trying to (   ) these (   ) communities to (   ) with each other.
     (isolate, collaborate, unite, use)

112

UNIT **14** DIALOGUE IN AN AGE OF CONFLICT

3. Extension

LISTENING CHECK

Listen to a talk and answer the following questions.

1. Which of the following communicative mode does the speaker compare "dialogue" with?
    a. Discussion
    b. Public speaking
    c. Negotiation
    d. Debate

2. According to the speaker, what is true about "smoking" nowadays?
    a. The number of smokers among young Japanese people is increasing.
    b. People in general are becoming negative about smoking.
    c. It is difficult to find a smoking-free building in Japan.
    d. The two opposing groups of people cannot discuss smoking in public.

3. Which of the following stance does the speaker take on "dialogue"?
    a. He is for dialogue.
    b. He is against dialogue.
    c. He is not sure about dialogue.
    d. He is not interested in dialogue.

4. Which of the following characterizes "debate" best?
    a. It allows multiple voices.
    b. It accepts contradictory arguments.
    c. It denies opponents' opinions.
    d. It makes their voices to be heard by others.

APPENDIX GLOSSARY

abduct　拉致する，誘拐する
a case in point　適例，好例
acculturation　文化的適応，文化変容
acquire　習得する，獲得する
adolescence　思春期
affect　影響を及ぼす
aggressive　攻撃的な
along the lines of　〜のように，〜と同様に
along with　〜と一緒で，〜に加えて
ancestry　先祖
anonymous　匿名の
appearance　風貌，見た目
application　適用，応用
appropriateness　適切さ
assimilate　同化する；同化させる
assumption　推測，予想
at first glance　一目見ただけで
at its face value　額面どおりに
attachment　絆，愛着
attain　獲得する，達成する
attention　注意(力)，集中力
authority　権威，威信；権威者
avoid　避ける
based on　〜に基づいて
be aware of　〜に気づく
be confronted with　〜と直面する
be free of　〜のない，〜から免れて
behave　（正しく）振る舞う
be in existence　存在する
be in their shoes　彼らの立場に立って
bother　悩ます，じゃまする
bring　〈価値などを〉取り入れる
bring to mind　思い起こさせる
bullying　いじめ
but to no avail　その甲斐なく
by all accounts　誰から聞いても
by means of　〜によって，〜という手段を用いて
call on　〜を訪問する

caregiver　世話をする人，介護者
carry out　行う
cheat　だます
cling to　握りしめる，捨てきれない
cognitive development　認知的発達
collectivist　集産主義
come prior to　〜に先立つ，〜より重要である
come to　〜するようになる
common values　共通価値，共通認識
communicative competence　コミュニケーション能力
complicated　複雑な，わかりにくい
component　構成部分，構成要素
composition　組成，混合物
conceal　隠す
concept　概念
conduct　行う
conflict　対立，葛藤
conformity　一致，相似
Confucianism　儒教
consensus　意見の一致，総意
consequence　結果，成り行き
considerable　相当な
considerate　思いやりのある
constant　絶えず続く，繰り返される
consultation　相談
context　コンテクスト，文脈，背景
contradictory　矛盾する，対立する
contribute　貢献する
conversely　反対に
convey　伝える
counterintuitive　反直観的
counterpart　相手
courtesy　礼儀
credibility　信憑性，信頼性
Critical Incident　クリティカル・インシデント，危機的事例
criticism　批評，批判

GLOSSARY

cross-cultural communication　異文化コミュニケーション
deal with　〜に対処する
deceive　だます
desperately　必死に
destination　目的地
detect　発見する,検出する
determine　決定する
detrimental　有害な
developmental psychology　発達心理学
dichotomy　二分(法),両分
dimension　次元
diminish　弱くする,衰えさせる
diplomatic　外交の
disassimilated self　異化された自己
disinterest　無関心
distinction　区別,識別
do harm to　〜に害を及ぼす
dominate　支配する
draw on　参考にする
dread　ひどく怖がる
due simply to　単に〜が原因で
dumbfound　唖然とさせる
eager to　〜しようと熱心な
ease the tension　緊張を和らげる
effectively　効果的に
effortlessly　楽に,努力せずに
embarrass　困惑させる,恥をかかせる
embarrassment　困惑,きまり悪さ
employ　用いる,採用する
encounter　出会う,でくわす
endorsement　承認,保証
end up　結局〜になる
endure　耐える
episode　エピソード,挿話的な出来事
epistemological　観念論的な
equip　備えつける,授ける
era　時代
establish　確立する,設立する
ethnic　民族の,人種の

ethnicity　民族意識,民族性
eventually　のちに,やがて
exaggerate　誇張する
examine　検証する,調べる
exhibit　表す,展示する
experience　経験;経験する
explicit　明確な
expose　さらす,受けさせる,触れさせる
falsify　論破する,偽る
feature　特徴
figure out　理解する
filial piety　孝行
foreign nationals　外国人,外国籍の人
-friendly　〜にやさしい,〜に使いやすい
fulfill　満たす
fundamental　基本的な,根本的な
furious　激怒して
gaze　見つめる,眺める
generalize　一般化する
genuine　純粋な,心からの
get along (well) with　つきあう
get in the way of　〜の障害になる
get one's meanings across　相手に真意を伝える
get used to　〜に慣れる
go parallel　同等である
go through　経験する;〈本を〉読む
governor　統治者,知事
hate speech　ヘイトスピーチ,憎悪表現
heritage　遺産,財産
hierarchy　階級組織,階級制度
hinder　妨げる,じゃまする
honorific system　敬語体系,敬語法
hypothetical　仮定の
identify　見分ける,確認する
immediately　即座に
immigrate　移住する
impede　妨げる,じゃまする
implicitly　暗黙のうちに,さりげなく
impose　強制する,強いる
imprint　刻み込ませる

improve	改善する，向上させる
inappropriate	適切でない
in a second	瞬時に
inattentiveness	配慮が足りないこと，無神経
in consideration of	～を考慮して
inequality	不平等
inevitable	不可避な
inferiority	劣等，下位
in harmony with	～と調和して
inhibit ～ from …	～に…させない
in light of	～に照らして，～の観点から
in one's eagerness to	～したさのあまり
in relation to	～と関連して
integral	不可欠な，必須の
integrity	完全な状態，高潔
intellect	知能，知性
intent	意志
intention	意図，意志
interact	意思を伝えあう，交流する；影響しあう
intercultural	異文化間の
interfere with	～の妨げとなる
interlocutor	対話者
in terms of	～という点で，～に関して
internalize	内面化する，習得する
interpret	解釈する
in the end	結局のところ
isolate	切り離す，隔離する
isomorphic attribution	同型帰属
join	合わせる，結合する
laborer	労働者
language acquisition	言語習得
likewise	同様に
lower-class	下層階級の
loyalty	忠誠，忠実
maintain	維持する，保存する
make a blunder	へまをする
monochronic	単一的に時間を使う〈文化〉
mother tongue	母国語，母語
multi-cultural coexistence	多文化共生
Muslims	イスラム教徒
mutual understanding	相互理解
neglect	軽視する，見過ごす
negotiation	交渉
no different from	～と全く変わらない
no exception to	～の例外ではない
no excuse	弁解の余地がない
no matter how ～	どれだけ～しても
non-linguistic	非言語的な（(nonverbalより狭義))
nonverbal	言葉を使わない，言葉によらない
norm	規範，規準
notion	概念，観念
obvious	明白な，すぐわかる
occur	起こる，発生する
ontological	存在論的な
oppose	対立する，反対する
orientation	方向性；方向づけ，オリエンテーション
originate from	～から起こる，生じる
otherwise	異なって，違って
outspoken	無遠慮な，率直な
overcome	克服する
overly	過度に
overwhelm	圧倒する
participation	参加，関与
pass on ～ to …	～を…に引き渡す
perceive	知覚する，理解する
perseverance	忍耐
perspective	観点，視点
phenomenon	現象
philosophy	哲学
play a role	役割をになう
plural	複数の
politeness	丁寧さ，礼儀正しさ，ポライトネス
polychronic	多元的に時間を使う〈文化〉
position oneself	立場をわきまえる
power-distance	権力の格差
practices	習慣
pragmatic	語用上の；実用主義的な
precisely	正確に，的確に
pretend to	～のふりをする
prevail	普及する，流行している

GLOSSARY

previous 以前の，先の
primitive 原始の，原始的な
principle 原理
priority 優先，優先権
procedure 手順，進行
productive 生産的な，充実した
proper 適切な，ふさわしい
prove 判明する；証明する
put effort to 努力する
raise 高める
react 反応する
realize わかる，気づく
recognize 見分ける，思い出す
refer to 〜に言及する
register 登録する
repetitive 繰り返しの
requirement 必要条件
resident 住民
resolve 解決する
resort to 〜を最後の手段にする
revitalization 復活
rude 失礼な
second language 第二言語
secure 確保する，守る
seemingly 見たところは，表面上は
sensitive issues デリケートな問題
set the stage 場を設ける，お膳立てをする
severe 厳しい，過酷な
sexism 性差別
show respect 敬う，敬意を払う
simultaneously 同時に，一斉に
sincerity 正直さ，誠実さ
Social Science 社会科学
socio-cultural 社会文化的な
solution 解決策
stance 立場，態度
stand out 際立つ
statement 主張，記述
stereotype ステレオタイプ，固定観念
straightforward まっすぐな，率直な

subconscious なかば無意識の，潜在意識の
submit 提出する
subside 和らぐ，落ち着く
subtle 微妙な，かすかな
superior 目上の人
superiority 優勢，卓越
supposedly いわゆる，〜と言われている
take initiative イニシアチブをとる
take turns 交替でやる
tend to 〜しがちである，〜する傾向がある
tentative 一時的な，仮の，試しの
term 用語
territorial 領土の
text messaging （携帯電話での）メール交換
theory 理論，学理
the ultimate goal 最終目標
transmit 伝える，運ぶ
treat 扱う
trustworthy 信頼できる，あてになる
underestimate 過小評価する，軽く見る
undoubtedly 疑う余地もなく，確かに
uneasy 不安な，心配な
unity 統一，一貫性
universal 万国共通の，広く行われている
unnoticed 気づかれない
upbringing 育ってきた環境，しつけ
update 最新のものに変える，更新する
utilize 使用する
utterance 発話，発言
value-laden 価値観を含んだ
value systems 価値基準
vary 異なる，一様でない
virtue 美徳
vital きわめて重要な，必要不可欠な
well-rounded 教養のある，幅の広い
What if …? もし〜だとしたら
when it comes to 〜について言えば
with regard to 〜については

編著者紹介

編 著

朴シウォン (Siwon Park)

神田外語大学外国語学部英米語学科准教授.

ハワイ大学大学院 Department of Second Language Studies 修了（Ph.D. in Second Language Acquisition）.

National Foreign Language Resource Center（米国），ハワイ大学，Kapiolani Community College（米国），霊山大学（韓国），神田外語大学 English Language Institute 等を経て，現職.

専門は，第二言語習得論，テスト理論，心理言語学.

共著書に『会話上手になるための 英会話の鉄則』（研究社），『Listening Expert』（The Japan Times）などがある.

共同執筆

杉田めぐみ (Megumi Sugita)

千葉県立保健医療大学健康科学部講師.

横浜国立大学大学院教育学研究科英語教育専攻，ハワイ大学大学院 Department of Second Language Studies 修了.

立教大学，千葉県立衛生短期大学等を経て，現職.

専門は，英語教育学，社会言語学.

共著書に『歯科衛生士教本 歯科英語』（医歯薬出版），『はじめてのアクション・リサーチ』（大修館書店）などがある.

小坂貴志 (Takashi Kosaka)

神田外語大学外国語学部英米語学科准教授.

デンバー大学スピーチ・コミュニケーション研究科修士号修了，人間コミュニケーション研究科博士課程単位取得終了満期退学.

モントレー国際大学（米国），立教大学を経て，現職.

専門は，異文化コミュニケーション研究.

著書に『異文化対話論入門』『異文化コミュニケーションの A to Z』（共に研究社）などがある.

Daniel K. Goldner (ダニエル K. ゴールドナー)

米国 Ferris State University 講師.

ハワイ大学大学院 Department of Second Language Studies 修了.

東海大学ハワイ校，Antelope Valley College（米国），高麗大学（韓国）等を経て，現職.

専門は，英語リーディングおよびライティング指導.

Life in a Multi-lingual and Multi-cultural Society
グローバル時代の異文化コミュニケーション

2013年11月22日初版発行

編著者
朴シウォン

著者
杉田めぐみ, 小坂貴志, Daniel K. Goldner

Copyright ©2013 by Siwon Park

KENKYUSHA
〈検印省略〉

発行者　関戸雅男
発行所　株式会社研究社
　　　　〒102-8152 東京都千代田区富士見2-11-3
電　話　営業 03-3288-7777(代)　編集 03-3288-7711(代)
振　替　00150-9-29710
http://www.kenkyusha.co.jp/

装丁・組版・レイアウト　亀井昌彦
編集協力　市川しのぶ
印刷所　研究社印刷株式会社

ISBN978-4-327-42191-5 C1082　　Printed in Japan

本書の無断複写（コピー）は著作権法上での例外を除き，禁じられています．
落丁本，乱丁本はお取り替え致します．
価格はカバーに表示してあります．

本テキストの文章・図表を入学試験問題に利用することは，著作権法によって認められていますが，同法に準拠して，本書が出典であることを，問題末尾に明記してください．